From Futility to Happiness

Sisyphus as Everyman

THE PRACTICE OF *A COURSE IN MIRACLES*

From Futility to Happiness

Sisyphus as Everyman

KENNETH WAPNICK, Ph.D.

Foundation for A COURSE IN MIRACLES®

Foundation for A Course in Miracles®
375 N Stephanie St, Suite 2311
Henderson, NV 89014
www.facim.org

First printing, 2008

Printed in the United States of America

Library of Congress Cataloging-in-Publication Data

Wapnick, Kenneth,
    From futility to happiness : Sisyphus as everyman /
Kenneth Wapnick.
        p. cm.
    Includes bibliographical references and index.
    ISBN 13: 978-1-59142-209-9
    1. Course in miracles. 2. Sisyphus (Greek mythology)--
Psychology. 3. Mythology, Greek--Psychological aspects.
4. Meaning (Philosophy) 5. Life. I. Title.
    BP605.C68W3533 2008
    299'.93--dc22   2008016202

CONTENTS

Preface

The original title of the 2003 workshop on which this book is based is: "Sisyphus: The Ego's Hero." The story of Sisyphus, incidental to Greek mythology, has long interested me, dating from my student years when I first read Albert Camus' profound essay, "The Myth of Sisyphus," which I will discuss in Part Two. As the reader can see from the book's subtitle, Sisyphus is all of us, for his life of apparent futility speaks to everyone—"No one but knows whereof we speak" (W-pI.182.2:1). Indeed, the theme of life's futility has run through our intellectual history from its beginning. It spans, for example, the ancient Greeks and Romans, the *Rubaiyat*, Shakespeare, and on to the modern-day existentialists. The late Carl Sagan's sage remark in an unpublished interview epitomizes this realistic view of human life. He stated that he believed that homo sapiens, like any other species, would become extinct. He concluded by saying there was no ultimate purpose here. This perspective is cogently summarized as well in the following pithy commentary from *A Course in Miracles* on our body's home: "…a dry and dusty world, where starved and thirsty creatures come to die" (W-pII.13.5:1).

Nonetheless, *A Course in Miracles* offers us another way of looking at our seeming fate, as did

Camus in his essay. Thus, through a change of mind brought about by a change in teacher, our lives of futility are transformed into opportunities of unlearning the ego's thought system. A purposeless life of inherent meaninglessness metamorphoses into a meaningful classroom that leads us home. It is my hope that this book, like the others in this series, "The Practice of *A Course in Miracles*," will be an aid in applying the Course's principles of forgiveness more meaningfully to our everyday lives, that they become increasingly happy and less futile in our experience.

The transcript of the workshop has been edited to be more reader friendly, and some questions and answers have been omitted when they were not germane to the book's theme, while others have been edited to maintain the flow of the written word. We have striven, however, to preserve the informal nature of the presentation and discussion.

Acknowledgments

As always, Rosemarie LoSasso, the Foundation's Director of Publications, has applied her invaluable editorial skill to the process of moving from the original workshop to the printed book, for which I am very grateful. My wife Gloria, in addition to being the inspiration behind this series of "little" books, was also invaluable in her editorial assistance. A simple thank you could never convey the depth of my love and gratitude for her support, and for being such an inspiring partner to me on this journey.

Introduction: The Myth of Sisyphus

We begin by placing the figure of Sisyphus in the context of Greek mythology. While not among the more important figures in mythology, he is certainly among the most interesting. He is most famous for the eternal punishment inflicted on him by the gods, the basis of this book's theme.

Sisyphus was king of the prominent Greek city Agyra, what is now Corinth. There are various stories about him scattered throughout Greek mythology, and he is also mentioned in Homer's *Iliad* and *Odyssey*. One of the legends depicted him as being a highwayman who stole and even killed. Most of the other stories, however, center on his tormenting the gods with his cleverness. In one legend, the river god Asopus pleadingly seeks King Sisyphus' aid in finding his abducted and beautiful daughter Aegina. In point of fact, Sisyphus does know the villain's identity and the daughter's whereabouts, but he wants something in return for his assistance. He therefore says to Asopus: "If you will create a spring for me so my people can have water, I will tell you where to find your daughter." Asopus agrees, and Sisyphus reveals that it was Zeus himself, the chief god, who took Aegina for his own, as was his wont with pretty young maidens who were ripe for his seductions. The mischievous king takes the crestfallen father to where Zeus is actively pursuing his pleasure. Preoccupied, Zeus had left his thunderbolts out of reach on the side of a tree. Asopus seizes the opportunity and threatens the god who flees. However, not to be undone, Zeus turns himself into a rock so he cannot be seen, and transforms Aegina into an island, so she cannot be found. Zeus then doubles back to retrieve his thunderbolts and hurls them at Asopus, who becomes crippled from the blows.

Zeus now turns his wrath to Sisyphus, and dispatches his brother Hades (lord of death) to take the rogue to the underworld as punishment. Yet when Hades comes to Sisyphus, he is greeted by the king's clever mocking: "How come Zeus sent you, the chief god of the underworld, on such a menial task? He should have sent Hermes (Mercury) instead." Succeeding in distracting Hades, Sisyphus then says to the god: "By the way, have you thought how you will take me down to Hades [also the name for the underworld]?" Hades replies: "I have these brand new handcuffs, from which you will not be able to escape." "Interesting," Sisyphus says, "How do they work?" Hades, already put off his guard by the clever Sisyphus, puts on the handcuffs to show his prisoner, at which point the impish king slams them shut and puts him in a closet.

Now captured by Sisyphus, Hades remains sequestered for thirty days, with disastrous consequences.

Since the god of death is in captivity, no one could die. People killed in battle return the next day to fight again, and this greatly upsets Ares (Mars), the god of war, who comes to Sisyphus and demands that Hades be released. Sisyphus has no choice but to let Hades go, and is thus to be taken to the underworld. But he is not finished with his schemes. Before he is to embark on what is meant to be his final journey, Sisyphus beseeches his wife not to give him a proper burial, which means not putting a coin under his tongue, necessary to pay the ferryman Charon who demands payment for taking the dead across the river Styx to Hades.

When he lands in Hades, Sisyphus seeks out Zeus' daughter, Persephone, who is also Hades' wife and goddess of the underworld. The wily Sisyphus beseeches her to right the wrong of his inappropriate burial: "Please let me return to earth. I will berate my wife for her misconduct having done this terrible thing, have her right the wrong, and then I will happily enter the underworld." Persephone feels sorry for Sisyphus and lets him go back, but of course he has no intention of returning to Hades. He thus remains in Corinth, enjoying his life, until the gods have had enough of his shenanigans and finally get him. He is now permanently confined to Hades, and his punishment is to roll a boulder up a mountain to get it to the other side, and just as it reaches the top, the huge rock rolls back down to the plain below. And so Sisyphus starts over again, and again and again—his eternal fate. In Homer's *Odyssey*, Odysseus visits the underworld, where he sees Sisyphus and describes him thus:

> And I saw Sisyphus at his endless task, raising his prodigious stone with both his hands. With hands and feet, he tried to roll it up to the top of the hill, but always, just before he could roll it over onto the other side, its weight would be too much for him, and the pitiless stone would come thundering down again onto the plain. Then he would begin trying to push it uphill again, and the sweat ran off him and the steam rose after him.

Another form of ironic cruelty imposed on Sisyphus by the gods was that the boulder was in the shape of the rock that Zeus had turned himself into to escape from Asopus. Thus, Zeus rubbed salt into the wound by saying to Sisyphus, in effect: "This is your punishment for taking the gods so lightly, and for being cleverer than we."

In a sense, then, Sisyphus is the perfect representative of the ego's thought system. He sins against the gods, and although he does not feel guilt—one aspect of the ego system he lacks—he is punished for his sin, a punishment that continues throughout eternity, his forever living a life in which there is no hope of change. Sisyphus has thus become a great symbol of life's futility, which is why in the original workshop I referred to him as the ego's hero. This, then, leads us directly to the theme of the first part of the book: life's futility. The second part will focus on the right-minded way of looking at our hero, the way out of his and our personal hell.

Part One

The Futility of Life

1. The Hopelessness of the Body's Life

There are many passages in *A Course in Miracles* that reflect to us the hopelessness of life in the body; a "life" that condemns us to death. No matter how we struggle to find meaning and purpose, to make something of ourselves, to find some crumb of happiness or peace, in the end it is for naught because we will die— just as, no matter how hard Sisyphus works to push the boulder up the mountain, it will roll back down. Actually, in some of the accounts, the rock rolls over him as it hurtles downward. Yet since he is already dead, he cannot die again. He simply repeats his endless task, sweat pouring off him and steam rising from his hard and futile work. There is no hope anywhere in such a world.

We begin with a passage that expresses one aspect of life in the world:

> The world you see is the delusional system of those made mad by guilt. Look carefully at this world, and you will realize that this is so. For this world is the symbol of punishment, and all the laws that seem to govern it are the laws of death. Children are born into it through pain and in pain. Their growth is attended by suffering, and they learn of sorrow and separation and death. Their minds seem to be trapped in their

brain, and its powers to decline if their bodies are hurt. They seem to love, yet they desert and are deserted. They appear to lose what they love, perhaps the most insane belief of all. And their bodies wither and gasp and are laid in the ground, and are no more. Not one of them but has thought that God is cruel (T-13.in.2:2-11).

We are all like Sisyphus in the belief we are being punished. While Sisyphus may not have thought like this, we certainly think—albeit unconsciously—that the punishment is justified because of our sin against God. This world and our physical life trapped in a "rotting prison" (T-26.I.8:3)—"the delusional system of those made mad by guilt"—is the fate of everyone who chose to listen to the ego's tale of separation: the individual existence that follows our seeming sin against God.

As Sisyphus sinned against Zeus and Hades, making mockeries of them, so does the ego tell us we have sinned against our Creator and mocked Him. In essence, we told Him that His love was not enough for us, His kingdom was not adequately satisfying, and we could do a better job of things than He had. Not only *could* we do a better job, we *did* do a better job. And so here we are, except that the guilt we feel over our perceived sin leads us to believe in our justified punishment. Thus, when the ego writes its script of separation, inherent in that script is punishment by

God for our sin against Him. When that thought system is given form in the world and body, we live a life as Jesus described in the above passage, one that begins in pain, continues with pain—both physical and psychological—and inevitably ends in death. We all "wither and gasp and are laid in the ground, and are no more." Thus the proof we have sinned against God by taking His life. Yet God has risen from the grave in which we deposited Him, and is hellbent on seizing back the life we stole from Him. And so we die.

There is a similar discussion at the beginning of "The 'Hero' of the Dream," where Jesus is a little more tongue-in-cheek, and obviously pokes fun at our bodily lives and the importance we give them—as if pushing a boulder up a mountain again and again is something significant.

(T-27.VIII.1:1-2) The body is the central figure in the dreaming of the world. There is no dream without it, nor does it exist without the dream in which it acts as if it were a person to be seen and be believed.

This, of course, was our big complaint against God. He did not believe we existed, and therefore our identity as a special self was invalidated. Telling God where He could go with His invalidation, we made a world and body in which we *are* valid. Everyone validates us, and so we are important, doing worthwhile things that are seen and appreciated, and thus our lives are significant. The passage continues:

(1:3-6) It [the body] **takes the central place in every dream, which tells the story of how it was made by other bodies, born into the world outside the body, lives a little while and dies, to be united in the dust with other bodies dying like itself. In the brief time allotted it to live, it seeks for other bodies as its friends and enemies. Its safety is its main concern. Its comfort is its guiding rule.**

So much for the seemingly great significance of our existence. Jesus is describing the selfishness and self-centeredness that characterizes our worldly lives, expressed in our special love and hate relationships that mirror our "original life" when we believed we separated from God. We cared then only about ourselves, and about preserving the self we had now established. As a result, we do not really care about others now; only about how they can meet our needs —whether our need to have a scapegoat (someone we justifiably hate), or someone who meets our physical and psychological needs, giving us pleasure and helping us avoid pain (someone we justifiably love).

(1:7-8) It tries to look for pleasure, and avoid the things that would be hurtful. Above all, it tries to

teach itself its pains and joys are different and can be told apart.

The confusion of pain and joy is an important theme in *A Course in Miracles*. In "The Obstacles to Peace," Jesus tells us that pleasure and pain are really the same illusion because they make the body real (T-19.IV-B.12). Whether we experience pain or joy, our egos experience them both as joyful, because if the body is real, the thought that gave rise to it must also be real, which means the ego is alive and well. Following its guidance, therefore, we never wish to look at the essential meaninglessness of what we do.

(2:1-7) The dreaming of the world takes many forms, because the body seeks in many ways to prove it is autonomous and real. It puts things on itself that it has bought with little metal discs or paper strips the world proclaims as valuable and real. It works to get them, doing senseless things, and tosses them away for senseless things it does not need and does not even want. It hires other bodies, that they may protect it and collect more senseless things that it can call its own. It looks about for special bodies that can share its dream. Sometimes it dreams it is a conqueror of bodies weaker than itself. But in some phases of the dream, it is the slave of bodies that would hurt and torture it.

This is our life here: futile and hopeless, and yet a life we try to make something out of. One can imagine Sisyphus, when the rock rolls back down, forgetting what has happened, struggling mightily to get the boulder up, with the expectation that he will get it to the top, at which point it will roll down the other side and his task will have been completed. With no memory of the past, he would feel that what he is doing is important, that there is something fulfilling about his task. This is our situation as creatures of this world. Over and over, we awake every morning to do the same senseless things, as Jesus just described in poking fun at our special relationships with money and with each other. Or, if you believe in past lives, that we return lifetime after lifetime after lifetime, trying somehow to make this work, having no awareness of its inherent meaninglessness. To the ego, life's meaningless nature *is* its meaning, and our unawareness keeps us trapped within its snares of nothingness.

In view of this, we can understand that one of the purposes of *A Course in Miracles*—made very clear in the early lessons of the workbook, for example—is to have us realize how meaningless everything here is so that we may cast aside our illusions that there is significance to our lives and what we do, so much so that even when we die, our accomplishments will live after us. We all desperately try to find meaning and purpose here, which is exactly what our ego wants us to believe in order to keep us motivated to push the boulder up the mountain. Again, our effortful activity ends up nowhere, but we are not aware of its futility.

Passages such as the ones I am quoting show how meaningless and trivial our lives are, for everything we do involves senseless things. Indeed, Jesus says "senseless things" three times in two sentences. And he is not just referring to the material things we strive after but do not really need. He is saying that *everything* here is senseless because the ego's purpose for everything is to keep us senseless, yet have us believe it all means something. Two lines that come at the end of Chapter 26 speak to the futility of our lives. Jesus is talking about a world of injustice, where someone wins and another loses:

> The world grows dim and threatening, not a trace of all the happy sparkle that salvation brings can you perceive to lighten up your way. And so you see yourself deprived of light, abandoned to the dark, unfairly left without a purpose in a futile world (T-26.X.6:2-3).

Thus our life; yet we try to enlighten it. Just as in a darkened room we flip a switch and a light goes on, so are we always trying to find a light-filled purpose in a life that is inherently meaningless and dark. Ultimately —and I am getting way ahead of myself here—the only meaning here is recognizing that there is no meaning. The only hope lies in recognizing there is no hope here. However, each time Sisyphus rolls the rock up the mountain he has hope, because he does not comprehend the whole picture, which is what Jesus attempts to help us do in his course; to see that the hero of our dream—the body—in its serial adventures just goes on and on and on: day in, day out; year in, year out; lifetime in, lifetime out. As Jesus says near the end of Chapter 19, when we choose not to awaken by passing through the ego's final veil, we "wander on, only to return and make the choice again" (T-19.IV-D.10:8). Each time we come back, we try to make life here work. People, including Course students, will feel that the fact there is something seemingly holy in this world, such as *A Course in Miracles*, gives life meaning. This misses the point, which is to teach us that *nothing* here is meaningful. This is the significance of the following from Lesson 189:

> Forget this world, forget this course, and come with wholly empty hands unto your God (W-pI.189.7:5).

We need to remember that nothing here is worthwhile, including this course. The value of *A Course in Miracles* lies only in helping us recognize that there is nothing worthwhile here. Otherwise, we condemn ourselves to a life of futility, struggling against the impossible, somehow believing we can conquer it, never realizing that the world is set up to be impossible; a place where things do not work forever. Moreover, the body was made to be an instrument that does not work perfectly; it is always breaking down, needy, in pain, seeking pleasure or relief from tension. The hopelessness of the body's life is apparent when we look at it from the Course's perspective. Each day we get dressed and groom ourselves, have breakfast, and proceed with our daily activities. The day ends and we go to sleep, only to awaken to the same routine. Thus we start all over again, as is Sisyphus' fate. The inherent futility of such a life escapes us. For example, the body never has enough food, oxygen, or water; psychologically, we never have enough money, safety, love, or attention. Indeed, the body was specifically made so that it would never have enough, for it is in a perpetual state of lack, always striving to push the boulder of life up the mountain. To counteract the monotony of this life, we developed a sensory apparatus and system of appetites that appear insatiable, enabling us to seek ever greater stimulation, innovation, and novelty through our special relationships.

2. Death

We turn now to two paragraphs in Lesson 163, "There is no death. The Son of God is free." Death, of course, is the ultimate proof of the inherent meaninglessness of everything here, even though we desperately try to pretend otherwise. In his book *The Denial of Death*, for which he won the Pulitzer Prize, Ernest Becker describes the many ways we psychologically seek to deny death's reality. Yet death, as is said in many different places in the Course, is the fundamental belief of our world (see for example, "What is Death" [M-27] and the current lesson [W-pI.163]). It is the final witness that proves that everything the ego taught us is a lie, for it strove mightily to have us make something significant of the world—to better it and ourselves—but in the end, everyone and everything in it will cease to exist.

(W-pI.163.2:1) Embodiment of fear, the host of sin, god of the guilty and the lord of all illusions and deceptions, does the thought of death seem mighty.

Death is the inevitable consequence of the ego's unholy trinity of sin, guilt, and fear; "the central dream from which all illusions stem" (M-27.1:1). Sin says we exist because we killed God, Who had to be sacrificed

19

so we could live: He dies and we live. This is our sin, which overwhelms us with guilt. The ego then tells us that God will rise from the grave and pursue us until He avenges Himself by taking the life we took from Him, leaving us for dead. Now He has life and we do not; He lives and we die. This is the thought system that made the world, and it is not difficult to see how the world perfectly embodies it. Everyone here sins because everyone here is selfish, caring only for his or her self, reflected in multitudinous acts of selfishness. We are all overwhelmed with guilt, not only for what we do to each other here, but for what we believe we originally did with God. We thus walk the earth, terrified we will be attacked and suffer pain. Whether this is actually true is irrelevant, for we will believe it because guilt over our perceived sinfulness demands punishment. Even if someone were acting kindly, we would easily distort it so that we could perceive that person as angry or punitive, thus fulfilling the fundamental ego thought of our being unfairly treated. This is why Jesus gives us this important line:

> Beware of the temptation to perceive yourself unfairly treated (T-26.X.4:1).

We need others to treat us unfairly for this means that *they* are the sinners. We thus successfully got rid of our sin by projecting it onto others, and so God will punish them instead of us. Moreover, on another level, their attacks on us prove that they are punishing us for our sin, which demonstrates that the sin of separation is a reality.

(2:2-4) For it [death] **seems to hold all living things within its withered hand; all hopes and wishes in its blighting grasp; all goals perceived but in its sightless eyes. The frail, the helpless and the sick bow down before its image, thinking it alone is real, inevitable, worthy of their trust. For it alone will surely come.**

Jesus says "*seems* to hold all living things within its withered hand" because what is truly alive cannot die. God has not been killed, and all that dies here is an illusion of life. Yet within that illusion everything dies, lying within death's "withered hand." Jesus is telling us that nothing here works and never will. The only thing we can know for certain is death. Recall the famous saying: "The only things certain in this world are death and taxes." Moreover, in this world we can be sure that we cannot count on anything or anyone; not even God, because the moods of the ego's God are so variable: if He likes you, He saves you; if He does not like you, He destroys you. Your fate does not really depend on you, but on God's whims. Indeed the book of Genesis relates two terrible incidents where God kills two people simply because He was "offended" by them (Genesis 38:6-10). Nothing, therefore, can be certain in God's world but that we can be certain about nothing—except that we will die.

We can depend on the certainty of death because we are certain that we exist. Whether or not we like ourselves or the world, whether or not we like the body—ours or another's—our existence is never open to question. For example, we see our image every morning in the mirror; our bodies get hungry and we feed them; we feel, think, and act. All that is certain. However, if our bodies are real, then, too, they are the embodiment of sin, which must also be real. It is a fact within the ego's insane world that our bodies came into existence because we separated from God and destroyed Heaven, and because we did, we deserve to be punished by death—the inevitable result of existence. Thus we cannot separate death from our life here. Yet to believe that death follows life is preposterous. But we do believe it, which is why Jesus tells us "there is no life outside of Heaven" (T-23.II.19:1). Everything in the world is merely an illusion or mockery of life, for it ends in death. However, how can life end in death if it is truly life? What God created is as eternal as He is. And *that* is truly certain.

(3:1) All things but death are seen to be unsure, too quickly lost however hard to gain, uncertain in their outcome, apt to fail the hopes they once engendered, and to leave the taste of dust and

ashes in their wake, in place of aspirations and of dreams.

Jesus is telling us that everything here is like that—since nothing works, nothing can be trusted. Yet what is most important is that we do not want to trust anything here, because not being able to rely on anyone or anything is what proves we are the innocent victims of other people's deceptions, cruelties, and injustices. If others are not to be trusted, it means we are victimized by what they have done to us. This establishes them as sinners, and us as the sinless ones. Therefore their guilt deserves punishment, while our guiltlessness merits salvation.

Thus, even though we may feel deep disappointment, we could not be disappointed if we did not want to be. After all, one cannot be disillusioned unless one first has illusions. This is why Jesus teaches that we want to be disillusioned, betrayed, and deceived, because that demonstrates our innocence at someone else's expense: *they* are responsible for our unhappiness, and ultimately for the very real separation.

(3:2-4) But death is counted on. For it will come with certain footsteps when the time has come for its arrival. It will never fail to take all life as hostage to itself.

Part One: The Futility of Life

Death comes to everyone and everything. With inanimate objects, like minerals, the disintegration or decomposition may take eons, but it will happen. It thus makes no difference whether we speak of a human life that ends at 20, 50, or 90 years, or a rock that ends its "life" in 90 million years, everything in time will come to an end. Some scientists, in fact, tell us that at some point the universe will implode upon itself and disappear. All this shows the inherent futility of "life" in the world. Indeed, no meaningful argument can be advanced from within the world's perspective that life is not absolutely futile and hopeless. As we will see later, Jesus says:

> Men have died on seeing this, because they saw no way except the pathways offered by the world. And learning they led nowhere, lost their hope (T-31.IV.3:4-5).

However, there is an answer, but not within the ego's system. Any meaningful argument has to come from outside the ego and its world, and this will be our subject in Part Two.

3. A Sorry Figure:
"Outcast, Homeless, and Afraid"

We turn now to Lesson 166, where we find a poignant description of what life is really like in this world. Very few people walk the earth with this awareness, yet, as we are taught in *A Course in Miracles*, if we look with open eyes on life in the body, this is what we would see:

(W-pI.166.4.1-3) Here is the only home he thinks he knows. Here is the only safety he believes that he can find. Without the world he made is he an outcast; homeless and afraid.

Jesus is speaking for all of us; if we were not in the body, living in this world, we think we would be homeless. We are thus terrified of leaving because this world is our perceived home, and this body is our self.

(4:4) He does not realize that it is here he is afraid indeed, and homeless, too; an outcast wandering so far from home, so long away, he does not realize he has forgotten where he came from, where he goes, and even who he really is.

Yet in truth it is our being bodies living in this world that makes us feel we are outcasts, for this is the source of our experiences of fear and homelessness, unaware that we are far from home, for its memory is buried in our minds. Jesus of course is not speaking of geographical distance, but of the ego's using its thought system of separation and sin to bury the thought of Atonement that would remind us of our true home and lead us there. And the ego's *thoughts* of guilt, fear, and hate are defended by the *world* of guilt, fear, and hate. There is in fact a home, but we have forgotten it, and therefore all we know is where our mendacious experience tells us we are.

As we will see presently, we are "a sorry figure" indeed, because we are outcasts here, and know only our homelessness with no hope of returning. Every time we think we have gotten the boulder of life to the top, it rolls back down. And so ours is an endless series of futile experiences. It is imperative for students of *A Course in Miracles* to understand that one of Jesus' principal purposes for us is that we recognize we are not at home here. Striving after things in this world—material or nonmaterial—gets us nowhere. Therefore, Jesus asks us to shift from directing our attention outward (the world) to inward (the mind). This is our only hope, and will be the focus of Part Two.

(5.1-3) Yet in his lonely, senseless wanderings, God's gifts go with him, all unknown to him. He cannot lose them. But he will not look at what is given him.

Here we see what I refer to as the ego's strategy. God's gifts are held for us by the Holy Spirit and His principle of Atonement, the memory of Who we are as God's Son who never separated from His Father. Yet we cannot look at the gift of Atonement because it has been buried by two layers, the double shield of oblivion that an earlier workbook lesson talks about (W-pI.136.4-5). The first is the mind's thought system of sin, guilt, fear, punishment, and death, all of which speak to the reality of the separation, denying the reality of the Atonement that says the separation never occurred. This thought system is then covered by the second shield, which is the world and body. Thus, we do not even know where to look, because we do not know we have a mind, having ended up as mindless creatures. We are therefore unaware of what is truly going on—just like Sisyphus who pushes his boulder up the mountain with no awareness that he has done this a quasi-infinite number of times, and will continue *ad infinitum* with no memory of what his life is like.

And so we keep secret the dark places of our guilt. The world—personal and collective—is a massive defense against dealing with what we believe to be our secret that we destroyed Heaven. We naturally do not realize that this secret is a lie, because we did not destroy Heaven. As one of Helen Schucman's poems, "Song to My Self," concludes:

> I never left my Father's house. What need
> Have I to journey back to Him again?
> *(The Gifts of God*, p. 38)

The ego thought system—mind and world—is all made up. Therefore, the ego's fundamental fear is not of God's truth and Love, but of the mind's power to choose to remember Him. God cannot be a threat to the ego because it knows nothing about Him. But it does know the threat of the decision-making mind that chose it, and can choose again, sending the ego back into "the nothingness from which it came" (M-13.1:2). As we read in the text:

> *Do not be afraid of the ego.* It depends on your mind, and as you made it by believing in it, so you can dispel it by withdrawing belief from it (T-7.VIII.5:1-2).

In summary, the thought we killed God and deserve to be punished is made to so terrify us that we are motivated to leave the mind through projection, making a body and world in which we hide to escape God's wrath, as Adam and Eve sought to do by hiding in the bushes. Yet the underlying fear remains—that if we ever returned to the mind and looked at the thought of separation, we would recognize its nothingness and choose again. Thus the double shield of oblivion (W-pI.136.5:2): First, the ego's terrible story of sin, guilt, and fear, in which we are the murderers, the sinful destroyers of Heaven who are terrified of God's punishment. Second is the mindless world of the body we made to protect us from the inevitable fate of destruction in the mind. And now mindless, we can never change our minds from the original decision, which remains seemingly forever. It is this motivation to remain mindless that holds in place the amnesia that prevents us from remembering how and why we made the world, and why we made it as a place of perpetual futility: birth, meaningless lives, and death.

We therefore strive to overcome the mindless futility of life here, desperately trying to make the world work, when it cannot. How could *nothing* work? Yet the ego keeps us trying, directing our energy and attention outward, away from the mind. We strive to make the body feel better—ours and our loved ones—and work to improve the world and its terrible conditions of suffering. And all the while, the inner world, which *is* the problem, lies buried beneath this double shield of guilt—in thought and in the world. Perpetuating this insanity, once again, is our need to keep buried our deep, dark secret. And so we all walk this earth—sorry figures indeed—with this guilty thought of having destroyed Heaven. As long as we fear this thought, we will be impelled to flee into the moribund world of bodies and remain there.

When we finally return to the mind and look at the ego's secret, we realize there is nothing there: we never sinned, and never fled to the world; there was no abandonment or betrayal, no loss or victimization. Only in the nightmare world of illusions did all this seem to happen.

Yet we will not reach that point until we plunge into darkness, walking with the Holy Spirit in "seeming terror" through the "ring of fear" (T-18.IX.3:7-9), realizing that the ego's dark, futile world is nothing because it comes from a thought of nothing. We shall return to this later: the way out of hell. But first we need be aware of what we are doing, which is why Jesus describes our life in this world. While more evocative in its language, the following description is not that different from what we have already seen in the previously cited passages:

(5:4) He wanders on, aware of the futility he sees about him everywhere, perceiving how his little lot but dwindles, as he goes ahead to nowhere.

Everyone knows death is the end, yet we strive mightily to deny it. We are not even aware that linear time is part of the ego's bag of tricks, and think we have real years and decades ahead of us. The workbook thus describes time as

      a sleight of hand, a vast illusion in which figures
      come and go as if by magic (W-pI.158.4:1).

Since futility is not something that happens at the end
—the ego's hell is right now—we are led to conclude
that we should eat, drink, and be merry, for tomorrow
we die (Ecclesiastes 8:15). Every time we choose to
believe in the body's reality, we are believing in death.
A Course in Miracles emphasizes that death has nothing to do with the cessation of physical existence, but
is an integral part of the ego's thought system of separation, guilt, and punishment.

**(5:5) Still he wanders on in misery and poverty,
alone though God is with him, and a treasure his
so great that everything the world contains is
valueless before its magnitude.**

    Since God's treasure is buried in our right minds,
we have no awareness of it. And identifying with the
ego's thought system—in the mind and body—we can
never remember that treasure. Indeed, the world's purpose is to cover the mind's thought system of guilt and
fear, which in turn covers the treasure of Atonement
and the mind's power to choose it. In its place, the ego
offers us its meager baubles of specialness: the substitute for love.

    The important section, "The Substitute Reality"
(T-18.I), discusses the special relationship as our

substitute for the reality that God gave us in our creation. We sought to substitute the love of the individual and the love between individuals for the Love of God that is perfect Oneness. Our special relationship with the ego was the first substitute for our relationship with God, and when that fragmented, we simply continued to substitute, thinking that this time we would attain the treasure and finally get what we want: this stock tip will pay off, this job or relationship will work, this doctor will help me, this new regimen will heal me, or this lifetime will do it. We are not aware that nothing will ever do it, because all things here are but substitutes for the true treasure of our Self, and thus they symbolize in form the original thought that we destroyed Heaven, murdering God and crucifying His Son.

Once again, we believe such insanity is reality, and therefore we run into the world of form and our various roles in the magical hope that this will stave off the anxiety of knowing we will be punished for our sin. And so, in desperation, we continue to try to make things work here, yet all that we do is simply attempt to suffocate this gnawing sense of guilt and self-hatred. We tell ourselves that one day something here will work: we will be successful and happy, and be seen as a good person. Underlying this, again, is the thought that we will never have to deal with the cesspool of guilt, terror, and hate in our minds. We are caught in a vicious circle from which there appears to be no escape.

(6:1) He seems a sorry figure; weary, worn, in threadbare clothing, and with feet that bleed a little from the rocky road he walks.

This is not the image we usually hold of ourselves. We do all kinds of things to conceal our mind's guilt, the gnawing self-hatred we all share. We cover over its overwhelming presence and attempt to make our bodies, personalities, and world pretty, seeking not to see ourselves as Sisyphus, pushing a boulder up the mountain again and again in a despairing display of futility.

(6:2) No one but has identified with him, for everyone who comes here has pursued the path he follows, and has felt defeat and hopelessness as he is feeling them.

We all have pursued this path and felt the inevitable defeat and inherent hopelessness of the body's life, entrapped in a world in which we do not belong. Jesus also speaks of this in a later lesson, which begins with his telling us how alienated we feel in this world that is not our home (W-pI.182.1-3).

It is thus imperative that we recognize what life in this world is like, otherwise there will be no motivation to seek the other way. We would simply try to make the best of a situation that is already hopeless, and continue to seek and seek and never find the answer. Each time we would get the boulder to the top, it would roll back down, our only hope being that it not roll over us. Again, nothing here works, and everything was made specifically *not* to work. Only love "works"; yet this is not of the body nor the world. Love can be experienced only through the mind's choosing to remember it. All forms of the ego's specialness but substitute for this perfect thought, and Jesus wants us to understand how totally hopeless all worldly endeavors are.

4. Seeking and Finding

We return to the text and "Seeking and Finding," a section that describes how the ego has us continually seek for what will make us happy, content, and whole, providing meaning to our lives. Yet we will never find it, for we all seek salvation from pain, whether or not we believe in religious systems. We can never truly be released from our suffering, however, until we get to its source in the mind, and then change our thinking. In other words, our pain comes from the mind's decision for guilt. Therefore, we need to return to the point of decision ("the point at which the error was made" [T-5.VII.6:5]) and choose again. Only then can there be real hope, ending life's futility, because we now seek for the answer in the one place it can be found: the mind. Our lives then take on real purpose, for seeking within means we will surely find life's meaning. This is precisely, again, why the ego made the world: so we would continually *not* seek in the mind, and thus never be able to choose Atonement—our only need.

(T-12.IV.2:1-2) The search the ego undertakes is therefore bound to be defeated. And since it also teaches that it is your identification, its guidance leads you to a journey which must end in perceived self-defeat.

This is another look at life in the body. The search the ego undertakes will never be successful because it is designed to direct us to search in the wrong place. We will never find happiness in the world, and if we think we have, we will be very much mistaken, for no worldly happiness will ever last. In Lesson 133, "I will not value what is valueless," one of the criteria Jesus cites to teach us the difference between what is valuable and what is not is that only the eternal is truly valuable. When we think we have something of value, he wants us to consider whether or not it lasts, like love and peace. Anything else is inherently valueless because it is not of the eternal God. Why, then, should we bother with it? The ego never wants us to understand that the only true meaning here lies in awakening to our real Self through forgiveness. Everything else is meaningless and without value.

Thus we need to ask ourselves: How many values that we pursue will help us awaken from the dream of separation? Almost all of them are designed to keep us from returning to the mind where alone we can exercise meaningful choice. Things here are geared toward keeping us asleep, not awakening. Even the most noble of purposes still ends up making the world and bodies real. For example, to end physical suffering in this world appears to be a noble and certainly well-meaning goal, but it will fail. The source of people's suffering, ultimately, is not disease or lack of food and water, but guilt, which comes from choosing the wrong teacher—in the mind, not the body.

This does not mean we should not help to alleviate suffering in the world's terms; but we need to understand that it will not truly work nor bring us peace if we believe in the *form* of what we are doing. Our bodies may be acting to alleviate people's physical suffering, but unless we recognize that the cause of suffering that we want to undo is separation, we simply become part of the problem. *Only the mind's decision for separation is the cause of suffering.* And so we need to learn that we are not separate from the people we are helping, or from those who may be hindering this help. Unless we proceed with this understanding, no matter how many baskets of food we donate, regardless of the money we give, we will not end the suffering. Thus if we do not undo the *cause* of suffering—the belief in separate interests—nothing will ever change; or if it does, some other problem will inevitably rise to take its place. Since we are seeking in the wrong place for the answer, no matter how well-meaning our solution, it will be wrong. This is why Jesus says:

> Trust not your good intentions. They are not enough (T-18.IV.2:1-2).

We continue with this theme:

(T-12.IV.4:1) Do you realize that the ego must set you on a journey which cannot but lead to a sense of futility and depression?

We all are like Sisyphus, on a journey that leads to a sense of futility and depression. No matter how mightily we strive to achieve our goals, we will never get the boulder over the mountain. Our failure thus means we will never find peace, salvation, or love here; we will never find our home. Trying to make the world's home better cannot make it work for us. Jesus wants us to understand that the ego's journey is one of futility and will inevitably lead to depression: in the end, we will always lose.

Therefore, if we are not painfully aware of this— and it is certainly a painful awareness—we will not be motivated to seek another teacher. We will think we are asking Jesus for help, but all we do is ask the ego, which cleverly masquerades as a wise teacher, having fooled Christians for over two thousand years. Again, there will be no motivation to ask Jesus—the true presence of love and wisdom in the mind—for help until we are certain that nothing here works, for we have been following the wrong teacher.

In recounting the story of how *A Course in Miracles* was written, it is important that we recall that Helen

Schucman and William Thetford did not know the other way, but they did know that the way they were following—projection and attack—was one of futility and depression, and was not making them happy. Their way was the equivalent of Sisyphus' pushing his boulder up, only to have it fall back down. Helen and Bill were experiencing the constant repetition of competitive feelings: hate, aggression, and condemnation—a veritable bottomless pit of judgment, with people always available to criticize and find fault with. Again, Jesus asks us to realize that the ego must set us on a journey that takes us only to futility and depression.

(4:2) To seek and not to find is hardly joyous.

We need to become aware that our lack of joy does not arise because we have not done a good enough job and can do better; nor is it that bad people have prevented us from accomplishing what we want. Our joylessness comes from our having looked in the wrong place for it—the body and not the mind. The other way of looking, of relating to the world, is not found in the external; only in the mind can real hope be found.

(T-12.IV.5:1-4) You *will* undertake a journey because you are not at home in this world. And you *will* search for your home whether you realize where it is or not. If you believe it is outside you

the search will be futile, for you will be seeking it where it is not. You do not remember how to look within for you do not believe your home is there.

This, once again, is the problem. We seek in the wrong place for answers because the ego does not want us to find them, and so we do not know that there is a place other than the world or body in which to look. All we know is that we are at the bottom of the mountain and have to push the boulder to the top. And so we push, and as we do, we make up stories—philosophies, theologies, mythologies, psychologies, and other "ologies"—to explain the significance, meaning, beauty, wonder, and spirituality of pushing a rock up the mountain. And as societies, we are quite ingenious and inventive at weaving these webs of spiritual, philosophical, and theological specialness to make sense of something that is inherently sense-less. We then spend centuries refining and debating them, proceeding to denounce, ostracize, and even kill those who disagree with us.

This is the point of these passages, where Jesus tells us, in effect: "Do not seek where you will not find. Do not try to make sense out of something that is non-sense. Pushing the boulder of seeming life up a mountain will not bring salvation, nor will it lead to truth or penetrate the mysteries of existence. The punishment inflicted by the gods on Sisyphus is a dream, and you need not continue its illusory existence." Who, then, are these gods but the made-up figures of the ego's dream of sin, whom we believe we offended. And what better punishment to inflict than a body that will die?—an absolutely brilliant plan on the ego's part; yet it is all nothing but a bad dream.

Anyone who thinks the biblical deity is the true God has not read that book carefully. He is a monstrously cruel figure who was so infuriated by sin that he made the suffering and death of the body as punishment (Genesis 3). The introduction to Chapter 13 in the text describes this insane belief system, as we saw earlier (see pp. 9-10). Moreover, it is not only our death we need to come to terms with, but everyone else's as well. This world of pain and death is not a nice place, and yet we keep seeking to make it work. Jesus' point, however, is that this is impossible.

We turn now to "The Real Alternative," which emphasizes the one true alternative in our seeking. The world offers thousands upon thousands of different possibilities for finding peace and happiness, yet all will fail us:

(T-31.IV.2:3-5) All its [the world's] **roads but lead to disappointment, nothingness and death. There is no choice in its alternatives. Seek not escape from problems here.**

Everything here leads to "disappointment, nothingness and death," and therefore it makes no sense to try to make the world pretty and holy. Once we seek escape from problems here, we may think we are doing something meaningful. But how can that be if there are no problems here to begin with? The world's purpose is to conceal the true problem of the mind's choice for the ego, a choice that antedates and transcends the temporal-spatial world.

(2:6) The world was made that problems could not *be* escaped.

This important line summarizes the world's purpose of ensuring that we never escape our problems—their source being the mind's decision maker, whose mistaken choice can never be undone by involvement in the external. The problem of guilt continually regenerates itself through projection, causing all kinds of misery and pain here. Yet we do not know where they really come from, which is why no earthly problem is ever resolved. As the workbook explains in two lessons (W-pI.79,80), no sooner do we solve one problem than another rises to take its place; no sooner do we solve the problem of hunger in the morning than we have lunch to contend with, then dinner, and sometimes snacks in between. Only to start over again the following day. Similarly, no sooner do we solve the problem of the lungs' oxygen

4. Seeking and Finding

depletion by taking a breath but that we have to breathe again; when we find those who love us and meet our needs, we continually strive to keep them from ever leaving us. We all endlessly repeat these cycles so that the problem of our underlying guilt is never looked at and thus never let go.

(2:7-11) Be not deceived by all the different names its roads are given. They have but one end. And each is but the means to gain that end, for it is here that all its roads will lead, however differently they seem to start; however differently they seem to go. Their end is certain, for there is no choice among them. All of them will lead to death.

No matter what Sisyphus thinks of his fate, regardless of how long he pushes, whether he does so with his left, right, or both hands; whether the rock faces front or back, in the end it will roll down and he will have to start all over again. Our so-called life always concludes in the futility of death.

(2:12-14) On some [roads] **you travel gaily for a while, before the bleakness enters. And on some the thorns are felt at once. The choice is not what will the ending be, but when it comes.**

The end is inevitable. Everything and everyone dies, whether of crib death or "natural causes" at 98. It does not matter whether or not our special relationships work. Since time is an illusion, how can the body's fate be important? From outside the dream, above the battleground of time and space, all illusions are the same, and all that matters is that we have made life *and* death real, thus rendering hope but a vain imagining.

(3:1-2) There is no choice where every end is sure. Perhaps you would prefer to try them all, before you really learn they are but one.

As all roads are the same, all the differing forms of specialness remain specialness: a meaningless substitute for love and a symbol of sin that demands punishment by death.

(3:3-5) The roads this world can offer seem to be quite large in number, but the time must come when everyone begins to see how like they are to one another. Men have died on seeing this, because they saw no way except the pathways offered by the world. And learning they led nowhere, lost their hope.

When we strive to find meaning here, when we do everything and nothing works, we inevitably conclude there is no longer a purpose in living, leaving suicide as the only meaningful solution within this insane thought system. Some, however, as we have seen, deny this logic and say: "Since nothing means anything, I might as well enjoy myself and not worry about the consequences; it does not really matter if someone gets hurt, for it is all meaningless anyway." Still others may say, more benevolently: "Even though there is no ultimate purpose here, we can at least live respectful of each other." Nonetheless, the meaninglessness of life remains the core of our unconscious experience. Incidentally, suicide is not only shooting oneself. Cancer, AIDS, and a heart attack are all suicide; so is "inadvertently" walking in front of an oncoming car. At least twice Jesus tells us that no one dies without his own consent, because the body and all its activities but reflect a decision made by the mind (T-19.IV-C.1:4; W-pI.152.1:4).

The ego, therefore, wants us to feel hopeless in a futile world. And so, rather than saying there must be another teacher or world we can live in, we believe this world is all there is. *Yet there is nothing here.* Holding to this thought, death seems the only answer, and it makes no difference if we come to this realization at the age of 20, 40, or 140. Only death is certain, the ego's ultimate proof that we lived, even if the life was of absolute futility and despair. Out of this hopelessness, however, we can reach a different conclusion: "There *must* be a better way" (T-2.III.3:6). But before we discuss this alternative, we need to consider yet one more aspect of the ego's hopelessness.

5. "Stabat Mater"

To conclude our discussion of Sisyphus' futile life and our own, I present Helen's poem, "Stabat Mater" (*The Gifts of God*, p. 92). *Stabat mater* in Latin means "the mother was standing," and can be traced to a medieval hymn about the sorrows of Jesus' mother Mary who stood at the foot of the cross. The first line of the hymn is *Stabat Mater dolorosa*: the mother was standing full of sorrow. It is a highly evocative hymn that stirs deep feelings in its listeners, and many composers have provided beautiful and inspired settings for it, such as Pergolesi, Palestrina, Vivaldi, Rossini, and Dvorak.

Helen's poem depicts the scene at the cross, except it is not Mary who stands in sadness, but all of us. Hardly a happy poem, it powerfully summarizes the futility of living in a world of crucifixion, a place of death from which there is no way out. Here is the opening line:

Who stands beside a cross is all alone,

The cross is the world, which reflects the ego thought that we have crucified God's Son by substituting our individual self for Christ, God's one Son. In *A Course in Miracles,* the term *crucifixion* is a symbol for the ego thought system: innocence beaten, tortured, and killed as sacrifice for us who are the terrible sinners. The ego tells us this is God's plan, causing His innocent Son to suffer for the salvation of the world. All the components of the ego thought system are here: sin, guilt, fear of punishment, sacrifice, injustice, suffering, and death.

This line tells us that we stand beside the cross alone, because we *are* alone. We desperately try to forge bonds with others, but cannot do so because it is our bodies, made to be separate, trying to join with other bodies, also made to be separate. Thus, at the same time our separated bodies try to prove another's is sinful and ours innocent, the other's body attempts the same thing with us. How, then, can there be joining? We are thus alone in this world, fervently trying to deal with the pain and anxiety of our solitariness. Again, each of us is alone because of the shared belief we destroyed Heaven; the pain of which we seek to conceal behind the veils of specialness and attack.

For sorrow such as this cannot be shared.

Although this is not the poem's explicit meaning, underlying these lines is the Course's teaching that we want our sorrow and thus do not want to share it. Our suffering means something has been done *to us*, the innocent victims of the sins of others. And if we can demonstrate this to the world, not to mention God Himself, we will not be deemed the miserable sinners who will be punished. Someone else will be so judged: the evil sinner who did this to us. This is why we all cherish our lives of pain, hurt, and loneliness; otherwise they—the scripts our decision-making minds have written—would not be as they are. Our lives, therefore, are purposive, for they allow us to point an accusing finger at another, saying: "Behold me, brother, at your hand I die" (T-27.I.4:6).

> **A pit is cut into the solid rock**
> **Between the world and her. No bridge, no hand**
> **Can reach across to comfort.**

We all seek comfort, but our only real comfort is in knowing our sins are forgiven. When we accept this happy fact, all pain is gone because it came from the belief we destroyed Heaven and thus deserve to be destroyed in kind. We deal with this terrifying thought by pretending it is not there. Thus denying its presence, we project it, making others evil. This is why *evildoer* is such a popular term these days: seeing the evil outside us proves our innocence—the ego's principle of *one or the other*. Yet this leaves us feeling all alone in the universe, separated by "a pit…between the world and [us]." We cannot be comforted, even when we consciously wish to be, because the source of our discomfort is not in the body or world, but in the mind. Our comfort, therefore, results from choosing differently, recognizing that our guilt is unjustified because nothing separated us from our Source.

Borrowing the famous phrase from John's gospel (14:18), Jesus closes the workbook, saying: "I will never leave you comfortless" (W-ep.6:8). The comfort he brings is that of knowing we are wrong; not only about everything here, but about who we are. We are children of Love, not sin and guilt. This means nothing has happened to change that Thought, which remains unbroken, unfragmented, and undivided. Perfect Oneness is still perfect.

Silently
She stands, without the bitter help of tears,
For tears were made for ordinary grief
Which long ago had come and been surpassed.

This is not ordinary grief, but the ontological sorrow we have carried throughout the ages. Buried in the recesses of everyone's mind is the horrid thought we destroyed our home and can never return. We desperately try to believe that God destroyed it, or others did, but the gnawing thought we can never truly escape is that *we* did this. And so our grief extends far beyond what can be assuaged by being held and comforted, told that everything will be all right. It *cannot* be all right as long as we believe we are here, as long as we open our eyes each morning to behold a separated world that proves our sin. Heaven is forever gone, and even if Heaven were to return, there is no way God would welcome us back. After all, our Creator knows that if He allowed us to return, our traitorous selves would sin again. And so there is no hope, poignantly expressed in Helen's poem.

We come to the second stanza:

> Here time is reckoned differently. A month
> Is held in every instant, and the years
> Pass by in grim procession in the space
> That others call an hour. Yet for her
> They reach into eternity.

We all stand at the foot of the ego's cross: a world of absolute hopelessness that transcends the transient pains of any specific moment, situation, or life. This is cosmic despair, born of time's grim procession of timeless futility:

> She stands
> Upon the edge of eons without hope.
> Here is forever. Here is timelessness.

This is not the timelessness of Heaven, yet it eclipses time's specific units. It is the ego's insane version of eternity that has us forever condemned to rolling the boulder up the mountain, only to have it roll back down. In this quasi-eternal dream of futility, we shall always stand at the foot of death's cruel and unyielding cross.

And now the poem's final line:

Who could believe the time of dying ends?

Who could ever believe there would be an end to this? Sisyphus is always pushing the boulder in Hades, the underworld of death; we are always in the process of dying. Indeed, as Freud observed, from birth we are preparing for death. "Who could believe the time of dying ends?" This thought, encapsulated in Helen's poem of despair, is the fact of life we desperately try to deny. We thus make a world in which we believe things will somehow work out. They never do, and deep within we know this because somewhere inside our minds we know we are trying to cover up this figure of the *stabat mater*, the guilt-driven mother who stands beneath the cross of death.

The beginning of "The Happy Learner" (T-14.II.1) tells us that the Holy Spirit wants us to see how miserable we are; otherwise He will not be able to motivate us to choose to learn His lessons. He therefore wants us to become happy learners, which occurs when we first recognize our misery and contrast it with the happiness toward which our Teacher leads us. It is imperative to see how miserable our existence is, even when it seems to work, which it often seems to do. In the end, however, all worldly experience comes to naught, for everything here comes to an end.

And so we all stand at the foot of the ego's cross, with no hope of our Sisyphean situation ever changing.

Q: Am I right in saying that nothing in the world has ever changed?

A: As we will see later in our discussion, there *is* meaningful change, but it is not on the level of the world. True change does not consist of making changes within the ego system, which, to use a popular analogy, would be the equivalent of rearranging the chairs on the Titanic. Why bother changing something that is doomed, let alone not even there? And so we do not necessarily change our special love or hate partners, but we do indeed seek and change the thought system that gave rise to this specialness—the cross of death—and in turn gave rise to the futility of Sisyphus' mountain and boulder. We can indeed try to make our lives better, as we all at times do, but ultimately our attempts will fail, which is why there is an inherent sense of disappointment, despair, and hopelessness here. Trying to make the dream happier, healthier, more prosperous, and less lonely will never succeed, for nothing in the world can bring us true happiness unless it is used to uproot the original thought that gave rise to the dream.

Although this sounds simple, and its logic cannot really be refuted, the problem in applying this principle is that our physical-psychological self is the product of this thought of separation. Deep down we realize that if we change the thought, our special self will disappear. Therefore, it is not that the ego does not want us to go back into our minds. *We* are the ego, and it is *we* who do not want to return to the mind. And so we choose a thought system that keeps us in a perpetual state of mindlessness, standing at the foot of the ego's cross where we worship the idols of evil, injustice, and death—the triumph of evil over good, which is the meaning of crucifixion. We then establish a theological myth that says it merely looked like evil triumphing, for in truth good won out over evil. Yet all this is done within the ego system, in which it is irrelevant if the ego's evil triumphs over the ego's good, or the ego's good triumphs over the ego's evil. All the while the non-dualistic Good remains outside the dream; the Good we are so terrified of choosing because within its omni-benevolence there is no good, no evil, no ego, no *I*.

Moreover, triumph of any kind expresses the ego's world of duality in which it makes no difference who wins. Whether God triumphs or the devil triumphs it is the same, because as long as there is a winner and loser we all lose, and it is the ego's thought system of separation that triumphs. We have taken the ontological thought of winner-loser, good-evil, victimizer-victim, denied its presence in the mind and projected it. And so we live in a conflicted world in which tension is the only reality. In any battle or war, therefore, *everyone* loses—individuals, groups, nation states. The only way to win is to rise above the battleground. Looking down, then, we realize that what happens below is unimportant, for the seemingly different sides are one: they both believe in separation. Thus, we all continually stand at the foot of the cross, all alone, filled with sorrowful tears that are beyond all tears; a time-less world from which there is no exit, for no meaningful change is possible in a mindless state.

Q: Does this mean that as a "good" *Course in Miracles* student I become one with my brother by recognizing we are stewing in the same pot?

A: Yes. As we begin to become more right-minded, we realize we are not alone at the foot of the cross. Everyone is there with us, for everyone worships the same slain ego savior, believing that good has been defeated by evil. The beginning of reversing this insane dream, of ending Sisyphus' dilemma, is in realizing there is another way of looking at it. What helps us learn is recognizing we are not alone. Correcting the poem's protagonist, we do not stand all alone. The truth is that we all share the same sorrow, which the ego does not want us to see. We are all Sisyphus, pushing the boulder up the mountain in an unending exercise in futility, believing we committed the same sin. We all did because God's Son is one. How, then, could we be alone, since we share the same ego? Regardless of our stance—good or evil— we are the same and therefore not separated. This reflects the truth that the separation is not real and never truly happened—we remain as God created us, and in that holy instant of recognition the cross disappears. Another of Helen's poems, "The Star Form," ends with the lines:

> There was a cross, but it has disappeared.
> There was a world, but there is only God.
> (*The Gifts of God*, p. 67)

Our problem, again, is that as separated selves we are part of the crucified and crucifying world, nailed to its cross. If that disappears, we disappear. That is our fear, which is why Jesus makes it clear that this process of undoing does not occur overnight. Since we believe we are time's creatures, we experience forgiveness within the illusion of time; our fear is born in time, as time is born in fear. And so the process of transforming and ultimately losing our self is a slow, steady, and gentle one in which we need not accept that we are not separate from God, for this thought is too terrifying. Rather, we learn to identify the cross in our lives without necessarily experiencing it as illusory. We need only open our eyes to the vision that everyone—*without exception*—is standing with us. We can indeed begin to learn that we are the same, for we all share the same interests and needs: the sameinsanity and despairing plight of living in a world and body in which hope is absent, and the same thought system of correction that we can choose—the other way.

6. There Must Be Another Way

As a transition to our discussion of another way of looking at Sisyphus, we will focus on the general issue of there being another way. We may not know the other way as yet, but standing at the foot of the cross, continuing to push the boulder up the mountain, there is a growing recognition that something is not right—there has to be something else to life. Pain has eclipsed our tolerance, and indeed has become so excruciating that we call out for help. There are some passages in the text that address this issue. We begin with the opening paragraph in "The Branching of the Road" (T-22.IV). Incidentally, the first two paragraphs of this section were not originally meant for the Course, but were part of a personal message to Helen and Bill in which Jesus asked his first two students to make another choice, as he asks us. It blended perfectly with the dictation and so they were told to keep it in.

(T-22.IV.1:1-3) When you come to the place where the branch in the road is quite apparent, you cannot go ahead. You must go either one way or the other. For now if you go straight ahead, the way you went before you reached the branch, you will go nowhere.

Think of the letter Y: a vertical line with a V atop it. The direction we have come from—the vertical—is our life. We stand now at the choice point where we realize something is wrong, and understand there are two ways of looking at this situation: the ego's wrong-minded way of separate interests, or the Holy Spirit's right-minded way of shared interests. As we will see later, the choice that confronts Sisyphus, and all of us, is not what we do with the boulder, but how we look at the situation. This is the branching of the road.

(1:4-6) The whole purpose of coming this far was to decide which branch you will take now. The way you came no longer matters. It can no longer serve.

The *forms* of our life do not matter, for their shared *content*—pushing life's boulders up the mountain of futility—do. Similarly, the color and shape of the rock are of no import; nor are the mountain's characteristics. What is essential, however, is that we have come this far so we can make a decision whether to continue on with the ego, looking through its eyes of judgment, or with Jesus and his vision. The roads of specialness we took to get to this point are now irrelevant. Therefore, despite our differing circumstances, we all share the same thought systems of crucifixion and resurrection, and the mind's power to choose between them.

Everything else is of no consequence because *form* makes no difference to the *content* of forgiveness.

(1:7) No one who reaches this far can make the wrong decision, although he can delay.

In the end, everyone will choose God, for the outcome is as certain as He is (T-2.III.3:10). Jesus' point to us here, as in many other places, is why delay? "Why wait for Heaven?" (W-pI.131.6:1; W-pI.188.1:1). Why choose to remain in hell when we could be home? Especially when we are already there, never having left.

(1:8) And there is no part of the journey that seems more hopeless and futile than standing where the road branches, and not deciding on which way to go.

Jesus was telling Helen and Bill, and all of us, that we do indeed have a choice. However, this choice is not what we do with the rock, but with whom we push it up the mountain; with whose eyes we look at our situation. *Not* making a decision, which in effect is making a decision for the ego, sustains the futility and hopelessness of our lives.

This idea comes through clearly in the passages we turn to now, revisiting Chapter 8 in the text. In the paragraphs we examine in the first section, "The Direction of the Curriculum," Jesus instructs us that we have two teachers that teach curricula that are opposite to each other: crucifixion and resurrection, pain and its release, attack and forgiveness, separation and oneness.

(T-8.I.4:1) Your past learning must have taught you the wrong things, simply because it has not made you happy.

If Sisyphus is not happy—and in the Greek myth he is decidedly not happy—it is not because of his punishment, but because of the decisions that led to it: trickery, deception, and mockery of the gods. His unhappiness is not a consequence of what he is actually doing, but the *meaning* behind it: his eternal punishment for sin. And so we are mistaken if we think that our unhappiness and sense of futility come from life's circumstances, for their source lies only in the thought system that says we deserve our miserable lot because we are sinners.

(4:2-3) On this basis alone its value should be questioned. If learning aims at change, and that is always its purpose, are you satisfied with the changes your learning has brought you?

Our learning has brought us proof that the ego is right: evil triumphs, good suffers; injustice is victorious and death wins out. Change to the ego always entails punishment for sin.

(4:4) Dissatisfaction with learning outcomes is a sign of learning failure, since it means that you did not get what you wanted.

Except what we wanted *is* what we got; what we think we did not want is what we truly want. We, as egos, want learning failure, pain, futility, and despair —what we believe we deserve. If it comes to us, we deserved it because of our sin; and if we sinned, we won. In this world, therefore, when we lose, our egos win. If God punishes us, we still win, because His punishment means we did in fact sin against Him: the separation is reality.

Our thinking becomes even more warped once we are enmeshed in this insanity: we won because of what we did to God, bringing our Creator to His knees and making Him as insane as we—the aforementioned second and third laws of chaos. We turn God into an enemy Who believes our insanity to be the truth: sinfulness and separation are reality, as are punishment and vengeance. Our fate of suffering, futility, and death—an oxymoronic life of death—thus proves that we defeated God. Jesus is asking us to be aware of our pain, the insanity that is its source, and to question finally if this is what we truly want.

We take a brief look now at some other statements in this chapter that expand this idea of learning failure:

(T-8.VII.8:1) There is nothing so frustrating to a learner as a curriculum he cannot learn.

It is indeed frustrating to be in a situation where we cannot learn what we want to learn. It is particularly so if someone stands over us who is impatient and critical. Children with learning deficits suffer this frustration daily, and if their condition is not diagnosed properly, it worsens because of the sense of impending failure. Jesus is telling us we are all susceptible to such frustration because we are deficient; not brain damaged, but mind damaged. The curriculum we want to learn is how to be happy and peaceful. Yet everything we are taught is designed to have us not be happy and peaceful, and therefore we inevitably fail in our learning.

(8:2) His sense of adequacy suffers, and he must become depressed.

We are depressed, though not necessarily clinically depressed, because this world is not our home. We wander aimlessly, continually pushing the rock of our burdens up the mountain of life, and then die.

(8:3-4) Being faced with an impossible learning situation is the most depressing thing in the world. In fact, it is ultimately why the world itself is depressing.

Like Sisyphus, we try to succeed in our tasks, striving to make the world work, but we fail. The ego teaches us to manipulate, seduce, and control other people in order to meet our needs and be happy. In our own way, we all become very good at this. Yet we are miserable. There are fleeting moments when the ego's plan of specialness seems to work, but they never last. And so, again, our world has been set up by the ego—the decision-making wrong mind—to produce learning failure, and a deep sense of loss, hopelessness, and despair cannot but ensue.

On the other hand:

(8:5-6) The Holy Spirit's curriculum is never depressing, because it is a curriculum of joy. Whenever the reaction to learning is depression, it is because the true goal of the curriculum has been lost sight of.

The true goal of the curriculum is not to have a happy dream in the world's sense, but to have the mind's happy dream of forgiveness. The Holy Spirit's curriculum is thus not to change the world—not to change the rock or appeal to the gods for a lighter sentence—but to change our minds:

> Therefore, seek not to change the world, but choose to change your mind about the world (T-21.in.1:7).

His curriculum is therefore joyous because it teaches us that we have control over our minds. This corrects the ego's curriculum of depression, which futilely sought to make the world work.

We return now to where we left off in "The Direction of the Curriculum":

(T-8.I.5:1-2) The curriculum of the Atonement is the opposite of the curriculum you have established for yourself, but so is its outcome. If the outcome of yours has made you unhappy, and if you want a different one, a change in the curriculum is obviously necessary.

Changing the curriculum means changing teachers. The ego's curriculum focuses on fixing things in the world and body, making the world's dream better: happier, safer, more successful—a place where there is no suffering and bodies are healed. The curriculum of the Holy Spirit, on the other hand, helps us awaken from the dream rather than strive to improve it. No joy is possible if the goal is world betterment. In fact, the world was made *not* to get better. As soon as Sisyphus gets to the top of the mountain, a force pulls the boulder back down, preventing it from going over the top and down the other side. Such is the nature of the world. Everything is pulled back down, for nothing truly works here: cars, houses, bodies, businesses, and families all fail in the end, for the existence of everything—

life and non-life—ultimately comes to an end. We desperately—in futility, hopelessness, and despair—try to have it be otherwise, only to have the rocks of our lives roll back down to the ego's ground zero of devastation and death.

(5:3) The first change to be introduced is a change in direction.

Jesus is really speaking of a change in teachers. The ego's direction takes us toward the body, maximizing its pleasure and minimizing its pain, even as it uses it to accuse others of sin. Jesus, however, uses the body as the means to return our attention to the mind, the home of real decision and meaningful change.

(5:4-8) A meaningful curriculum cannot be inconsistent. If it is planned by two teachers, each believing in diametrically opposed ideas, it cannot be integrated. If it is carried out by these two teachers simultaneously, each one merely interferes with the other. This leads to fluctuation, but not to change. The volatile have no direction.

An example of this wrong-minded attempt to compromise reality and illusion is asking Jesus to help us make the dream better. If the direction of the curriculum is to move us back to the mind, and we have our spiritual teacher focus on bodies—personal or collective—or on relationships between them, we are demonstrating the mistake Jesus is describing: taking two teachers who are teaching contradictory things, and trying to forge an alliance that makes it appear that they say the same thing. Clearly at this point each interferes with the other, and only the ego's curriculum survives. Jesus tells us earlier in the text:

> The way out of conflict between two opposing thought systems is clearly to choose one and relinquish the other (T-6.V-B.5:1).

The ego, again, seeks to have us choose both systems, attempting to blend them in the strange effort to reconcile the irreconcilable division between form (body) and content (spirit) that we find in formal religions. Thus Jesus cautions us:

> Formal religion has no place in psychotherapy, but it also has no real place in religion. In this world, there is an astonishing tendency to join contradictory words into one term without perceiving the contradiction at all. The attempt to formalize religion is so obviously an ego attempt to reconcile the irreconcilable that it hardly requires elaboration here (P-2.II.2:1-3).

This means that once we formalize the authentic religious experience or spiritual teaching, we lose its essence. Speaking of the ego's specialness, Jesus tells us that the special relationship is a triumph of form over content (T-16.V.12-13). If we go beneath the surface meaning of the words, we can see in that section, "The Choice for Completion," Jesus is speaking of Christianity, which tried to formalize love in ritual and dogma, thus triumphing over its content.

We can therefore understand, from the point of view of *A Course in Miracles*, how religions of the world have taken the original message of the "founder" and distorted it in the service of the ego. This is inevitable. The ego is terrified of love and truth, and to the extent that we identify with its thought system of guilt and fear, which we do almost all the time, God's truth and Love will be perceived as threatening and fearful. The ego, therefore, cleverly devises the strategy of *if you can't lick 'em, join 'em*: it joins the truth, but changes it. The love that inspired the enlightened ones who are the source of the religion is met by the fear of those who follow them. They cannot but project their egos onto the egoless teaching, thus making form and ritual ends in themselves, rather than means to reach the End. What then becomes important is not the inspirational truth, but the preservation of this truth in form. Codifications of the teaching, which are really obfuscations, must follow, and before we know it we have the idols of specialness worshiped in the form of special people, rituals, objects, places, and so on. This is inevitable with *A Course in Miracles*, too, as we can already see beginning to happen.

(5:9) They cannot choose one because they cannot relinquish the other, even if it does not exist.

Even though the ego does not exist, we cannot let it go because to do so means we let go of ourselves—the greatest fear of the individual, special self.

(5:10) Their conflicted curriculum teaches them that *all* directions exist, and gives them no rationale for choice.

This is the situation in a dualistic system. God is present in the world and so all directions seem to exist —to the mind, and away from it to the body. Yet they cannot both be true: we cannot have a little bit of Heaven in hell, or hell in Heaven (M-13.7:1-5). Either truth *or* illusion is true, but not both of them—love and hate, oneness and separation, light and dark do not coexist. It is *one or the other*, and in the end we must choose truth and let illusion go.

One of the purposes of *A Course in Miracles* is to set the record straight, with Jesus saying, in effect: "What you have been taught for two thousand years is not what I said. Even if you got the words right, itself highly doubtful, the meaning certainly was wrong. Do not confuse me with the ego, for I am not asking you to live a happier dream." As he said to Helen in the prose poem, "The Gifts of God": "I am not a dream that comes in mockery" (*The Gifts of God*, p. 121).

Jesus is not part of our dream that mocks God, for he is not a body but a thought—as we are. He tells us in the text:

> Thought cannot be made into flesh . . . (T-8.VII.7:4).

Spirit cannot come into the body, and we must choose which is to be our reality.

(6:1) The total senselessness of such a curriculum must be fully recognized before a real change in direction becomes possible.

We need to recognize the futility of pushing the boulder of specialness up the mountain, trying to make our world work and achieve happiness here. Such goals will fail, for the only happiness possible in the world is learning that we are not *of* the world. Thus if we do not realize the inherent nothingness of the ego, we can never choose against it. Without recognizing the hopelessness of its thought system, the ego will remain. This is when we bring God into the world, asking Jesus for help to return home to Him, while all we really do is ask "God" to help us build a happier kingdom *here*, away from Him.

(6:2-4) You cannot learn simultaneously from two teachers who are in total disagreement about everything. Their joint curriculum presents an impossible learning task. They are teaching you

entirely different things in entirely different ways, which might be possible except that both are teaching you about yourself.

We cannot learn to return to Heaven while we build a home here. We cannot learn that our identity is spirit when we are taught that our identity is physical. *A Course in Miracles* is a non-dualistic system, and dualistic systems teach contradictory things: the coexistence of spirit and flesh, good and evil, Heaven and hell. The curriculum with this Teacher is different, for we are learning that there can be no compromise between truth and illusion. This means we cannot be a son of the ego *and* a Son of God, a son of separation *and* a Son of perfect Oneness.

(6:5) Your reality is unaffected by both, but if you listen to both, your mind will be split about what your reality is.

This, of course, is the problem, for we think we are both spirit and flesh. The integration of mind, body, and spirit is impossible according to *A Course in Miracles*. The mind is not in the body, which is but a projection of the mind, and *ideas leave not their source*: the *idea* of separation has never left the mind that is its *source*. Moreover, spirit is beyond mind *and* body, and has nothing to do with either. Thus it cannot be integrated: thought cannot be made flesh, and spirit

72

cannot incarnate. Once again, we cannot return home and awaken from the dream while we seek to build a better home in the dream. How can we learn of the Holy Spirit's happy dreams, which will lead us out of the world, when our eyes are fixed on the ego's happy dreams in the world? We must indeed choose one or the other.

The focus of Part Two is on what happens when we make the right choice and choose the right teacher. We will return to Sisyphus, understanding that there is another way to approach his—and our—existential dilemma.

Part Two

A Right-Minded Sisyphus

7. Introduction:
"One Must Imagine Sisyphus Happy"

We now address Sisyphus and his fate from a right-minded point of view. The inspiration for this different way of looking comes from Albert Camus (1913-1960), the famous French philosopher and writer (he was actually Algerian). In addition to being a profound thinker, Camus was a wonderful writer and won the Nobel Prize for literature, having written three novels—*The Stranger*, *The Plague,* and *The Fall* (all metaphorical presentations of his thinking)—and a series of plays, short stories, and essays.

Though Camus was an avowed atheist, there is a spirituality that flows throughout his work, which will be clear from my remarks below. Arguably his most important essay is "The Myth of Sisyphus," which although he includes an appendix on the Greek myth, is not really about Sisyphus at all. The essay opens with Camus stating that the only serious philosophical problem is that of suicide. In talking about the state of the world, he frequently used the word *absurd*, which denotes the essential meaninglessness and senselessness of life. This philosopher's response to the absurd was that suicide was not the answer. Indeed, there *is* meaning in the world if one is conscious of life's absurdity, for it is one's struggle against this human condition that makes life meaningful. What interested Camus in the myth was the period during which Sisyphus walked down the mountain after laboring mightily to get the boulder to the top, only to have it roll back down. Camus' hero was able to become fully conscious of the futility of what he was doing and the absurd nature of the world, thus transcending his fate. He therefore became free, leading Camus to end his essay by writing: "One must imagine Sisyphus happy."

From the point of view of *A Course in Miracles*, Sisyphus is happy because he is able to look at the absurd futility of his life without depression or despair. This right-minded looking opens the mind, enabling one to understand this is all a dream. And so we do not fight against the dream, rant and rave about its unfairness, or try to change or deny it. We simply accept the dream's intrinsic nature, *yet knowing it remains a dream*. It therefore is not good or bad—a dream is a dream, an illusion is an illusion—and this enables us at last to transcend it and return to the mind. This is the other way Jesus holds out to us. To quote the important line again:

> Therefore, seek not to change the world, but choose to change your mind about the world (T-21.in.1:7).

We do not seek to alter our fate of living in a futile world in which there is no hope and nothing can ever change. Instead, we work on changing our minds about it. In other words, we do not give the world power to take away the love and peace that is in our right minds.

Camus' Sisyphus was happy because he did not give his fate power over him, and thus was able to rise above it. While Camus never specifically said this, we can infer from his statement that the worldly (godly or otherwise) powers could do whatever they chose to his body, but they could not affect his mind. That attitude is no different, for example, from that of Victor Frankl, the psychiatrist who endured the concentration camps in World War II, lost his family and work—they burned his manuscripts—but emerged a much stronger person because he realized that no matter what the Nazis did, they could not change *him*. They could affect his body and the bodies of his loved ones, but not his mind. Thus the perception of his "enemies" inevitably changed. When we allow ourselves to rise above the battleground to where Jesus is, and then look back down with him, we see everything differently. Things are indeed terrible on the battleground: bodies strewn everywhere, sometimes winning, other times losing; but in the end everyone dies, which means everyone loses. Again, there is no hope, for the finiteness of life is its futility.

Yet above the battleground we are masters of our fate. Perhaps we are not masters of the body's "natural laws," or what other bodies do, but we *are* in control of our minds. Herein lie our power, freedom, and joy. What makes us happy dreamers is that we recognize that the world is a dream.

Repeating the main point, no one can be truly happy in this world because it is not home. All who come here are aliens and outcasts, sorry figures wearing threadbare clothing (W-pI.166.6:1), desperately trying to make sense out of a world that is inherently senseless, striving to derive meaning from pushing a rock up a mountain only to have it fall back down. However ingenious we may be in attempting to make sense of this—theologically or otherwise—in the end, life remains inherently meaningless. However, what does give it meaning is seeing that it affords us the opportunity of learning this is a dream from which we can awaken. This power is the nature of true freedom —not freedom of the body, or freedom within the world, but freedom to rise above it. Nothing here has power over the mind, nor can anything prevent us from returning—in what *A Course in Miracles* refers to as the holy instant—to the decision maker that can choose Jesus as its teacher instead of the ego.

This is why Sisyphus can be happy. He can shift attention to his mind and walk down the mountain, recognizing that he cannot change his fate. The judges in Hades spoke, but he ended up having the last laugh. He outsmarted them when he was alive, and outsmarts them in his death because they no longer have power over him. His true imprisonment lay in thinking they did, by virtue of the punishment they inflicted on him. Yet by rising above *their* battleground and not letting it affect him—realizing he is not the body pushing up the rock—he becomes free. In effect, this is Jesus' Sisyphean message to us in his course, that we turn the tables on the ego forces in the world, whether their physical embodiments or the thought system itself. None of them has power over us unless we give it to them. In other words, the ego has no power unless we put air in its balloon and make it seem to be something it is not. This is salvation's secret, as Jesus tells us in the text:

> The secret of salvation is but this: that you are doing this unto yourself. No matter what the form of the attack, this still is true. Whoever takes the role of enemy and of attacker, still is this the truth. Whatever seems to be the cause of any pain and suffering you feel, this is still true. For you would not react at all to figures in a dream you knew that you were dreaming. Let them be as hateful and as vicious as they may, they could have no effect on you unless you failed to recognize it is your dream (T-27.VIII.10).

In the mid-1960s I was on a civil-rights march in Mississippi, led by Martin Luther King, Jr. It was in response to the shooting of James Meredith, and Dr. King wisely turned the event into a voter-registration march. He spoke one evening in a church to a group of Mississippi blacks, and his message was clear: "They (the whites) cannot break your back unless it is bent. No matter what your oppressors have done or continue to do, they cannot truly persecute or victimize you unless you let them do it. Only if you bend your back can they break it." Specifically, Dr. King was telling his followers that they should register and vote, thereby gaining power in the state. And sure enough, many black legislators were voted in. His message is familiar. Again, no matter what people do to our bodies, it can have no effect on our peace unless our decision-making minds give away their power. Our only hope to be happy in this world is to realize that it has no power to give us peace or take it from us. We need not necessarily accept the Course's metaphysical teaching that the world is not even here. It is enough to say that nothing in the world can make us happy or unhappy. Our minds alone are the power behind the world's thrones of specialness. Recall these lines from the workbook:

The seeming cost of accepting today's idea ["My salvation comes from me"] is this: It means that nothing outside yourself can save you; nothing outside yourself can give you peace. But it also means that nothing outside yourself can hurt you, or disturb your peace or upset you in any way. Today's idea places you [the decision-making mind] in charge of the universe, where you belong because of what you are (W-pI.70.2:1-3).

We turn now to a fuller discussion of returning to the power of decision that is present in the mind, Jesus' goal for us in *A Course in Miracles*.

8. "Choose Once Again"

The following passage from Helen's prose poem "The Gifts of God" (*The Gifts of God*, pp. 117-18), originally a message from Jesus to Helen, will serve as an introduction to this section:

"Choose once again" is still your only hope. Darkness cannot conceal the gifts of God unless you want it so.

There is no hope in the world, since it is a place of fear, pain, and death. Hope lies only in the mind's choosing differently. The darkness of the ego's thought system, as well as its worldly embodiment, cannot cover the gifts of God in our minds unless we want the darkness to cover these gifts. Only we have the power to cover them, not the world. We simply invite the world to do our bidding—protecting us from God's gifts—and it is more than happy to oblige. Our Creator's "gift" is the Atonement, the Presence of the Holy Spirit that says the separation never happened. God's Love is as fully present to us as it was before the separation, *because there was no separation*—we still remain at one with His Love. Thus the Atonement could be seen, metaphorically, as the ultimate of God's gifts, over which the darkness has no power unless, once again, our minds choose to give it power to conceal His Love.

In peace I come, and urge you now to make an end to time and step into eternity with me. There will not be a change that eyes can see, nor will you disappear from things of time.

Sisyphus may still be rolling his stone up the mountain—"There will not be a change that eyes can see, nor will you [your body] disappear from things of time"—but he looks at his life through the eyes of vision and so his attitude changes, demonstrating the power he has over his mind. Indeed, *A Course in Miracles* is solely about returning to our awareness the power of our minds to choose. So much of our time is spent trying to fix our and other people's lives that we forget that all we ever have to fix is our distorted thinking, and all we need change is our teacher—the meaning of "choose once again." Jesus therefore asks us to choose whether to have him as our mentor or the ego. Since we had first chosen the ego, we need to choose differently.

This relieves us of a tremendous burden, for we need no longer struggle against the world. We simply continue as we have been doing, without opposition —without anger, hate, or criticism of others or ourselves. We need to realize that we cannot be expressions of love in this world if we believe we are doing something holy, spiritual, or meaningful. The only meaningful thing we can do is choose again, for then the love we choose flows through our minds to direct the body. Thus we may behave like "do-gooders," but with the awareness that we are not the ones doing the good—it comes through us—and so there is no investment in the outcome, in people accepting our gifts, love, or generosity. We realize everything here is an illusion. Yet love, which can be expressed in the dream, is not an illusion, and takes whatever form is most helpful in the world of form, which again, is not our concern.

Therefore, it makes no difference whether we futilely push a stone up a mountain, or sit in a palace at the foot of the mountain. There is no hierarchy of illusions—an illusion is an illusion is an illusion. Repeatedly struggling with the stone, or basking in a palatial residence, we still believe we are bodies. It is *how* we live in the body that is important, which really means *with whom* our minds live. We thus can be miserable in the palace and happy pushing the rock, or miserable pushing the rock and happy in the palace. Our happiness has nothing to do with the circumstances. To repeat, we cannot be of help if it is the ego doing the helping. This means that our only focus should be not on what is going on around us, but only on getting our ego out of the way. And so we remain vigilant for its thought system, bringing it to the Holy Spirit in our minds. In other words, we "choose once again." This, our only interest, allows Jesus' vision to be the eyes through which we perceive all our situations; the meaning of what he says next:

But you will hold my hand as you return because we come together.

If Sisyphus is aware that Jesus is pushing the boulder up the mountain with him, he will not care about what happens to it; whether it goes over the top or rolls back down. What difference could it make if his focus is only on the love in his mind, not the body's activity? What makes this difficult is that we underestimate the extent of our bodily identification, how inextricably linked we are with this physical, psychological self we believe is our identity. Therefore, when we think of Jesus, it is tempting to think of him pushing the boulder with us—literally—instead of being in our minds as we push the boulder. This is a huge difference. We would actually think we would be better off *not* pushing the boulder up, believing it is silly and pointless to be doing this when we could, for example, be helping people instead. Yet how would we know? How could anyone truly know the benefit of what is done? While I am not encouraging people to find a mountain and push a meaningless rock to its top, if that is the curriculum of our dream, we should do it; the crucial thing being that we take Jesus' hand as we do so.

Now the hosts of Heaven come with us, to sweep away all vestiges of dreams and every thought that rests on nothingness.

The "hosts of Heaven" refers to God's Love in our minds. And "every thought that rests on nothingness" means every ego thought that finds expression in this world.

How dear are you to God, Who asks but that you walk with me and bring His light into a sickened world which fear has drained of love and life and hope.

Jesus is not talking about doing things in a nonexistent world. Rather, we bring light into a sickened world because the world is in our minds. Choosing to be right-minded, the light of Atonement flows through our healed mind into the projected world, illuminating all that seems external. Since this has nothing to do with our special self that seeks to do special things, our only need is to get the ego out of the way. Our sane friend Sisyphus would thus not bemoan his cruel fate—after all, he could have said to the gods: "I was only kidding. You do not have to make a big deal out of a silly, practical joke"—but simply change his mind.

Surely you will not fail to hear my call, for I have never failed to hear your cries of pain and grief...

Jesus hears our cries of pain and grief, and helps us recognize that they are not a result of external conditions. If they were, he could not help us. Suffering does not come from situations in which we find ourselves —the "terrible" people with whom we are involved, or the "wonderful" people who end up being terrible— but arises only when we exclude Jesus. Therefore, including him undoes our pain. And so, what we need do, day in and day out, is to be aware of how quickly we give away our power to circumstances and relationships we believe can deprive us of peace and happiness, or provide them; how quickly we place our pains and joys outside ourselves and make them specific. Such projection is the real cause of our discomfort and hopelessness, and not what appears to be external. Everything we do here is futile because, as we have seen, everything dies; we can depend on nothing in the world, despite what seems to be the case. As we read in the text:

> Nothing so blinding as perception of form (T-22. III.6:7).

Perception lies. The world of form deceives, for it keeps us mindlessly unaware of our mind's content:

Jesus' love that reflects Heaven's truth, or the ego's llusory fear.

…I have come to save and to redeem the world at last from fear. It never was, nor is, nor yet will be what you imagine.

Jesus redeems the world from fear because fear is in the mind, and when we bring this fear to his love, the fear is gone. Thus fear never was, is not, and will never be what we think. Experience tells us we are afraid of something external: getting sick, dying, losing a loved one, war, being fired, or the weather. Yet fear is never of these things; how can an illusion be frightening? Recall the line: "I am not a dream that comes in mockery" (*The Gifts of God*, p. 121). The world's Jesus is the one who came in mockery, for he made the world and body real, thus mocking God and His perfect Son. Jesus, therefore, does not remove our problems; he does not assure Sisyphus he will take care of things. Rather, he helps his brother realize that his circumstances are nothing. "What difference does it really make if you endlessly push a boulder up and down, or if you are back in Corinth as king? All that matters is whether you let my love be your companion." This is the only lesson we need learn. Instead of striving mightily to fix our world, bringing Jesus into it to help us, we bring our world to him. What needs fixing is simply that we have kept it from him, and bringing our world to him that our minds may look at it together is the answer. He then says to us:

Let me see for you, and judge for you what you would look upon. When you have seen with me but once, you would no longer value any fearful thing at cost of glory and the peace of God.

Jesus asks us to think of the cost of excluding him, making the world of suffering real, whether our own or another's. It is costing us the glory and the peace of God. "Is that what you want?" he asks. "You think you are being loving, kind, and helpful, but when you push me away, these traits are impossible for you to experience, and so how could you be loving, kind, and helpful to others? Focus only on the love within you, letting me be your eyes so you may judge with me what you would look upon." *We* judge by evaluating the world as good or bad. For example, remaining king of Corinth is good; pushing a rock up a mountain is bad. Yet in truth neither is good or bad, for they are but opportunities to learn what is truly good and bad: choosing Jesus as our teacher is good because that brings happiness to us and others; choosing the ego is bad because it causes pain. Such understanding is the vision he asks us to choose until all choice ends in the blazing light of Atonement.

Thus our first response is almost always to change the situation instead of our internal state. While this does not mean we are not to act in the world, or even seek to change things here—our personal world or the world at large—it does mean that if we do not go within first, it will be our egos attempting to effect the change, and then the problem will never be resolved.

We now turn to Lesson 191, "I am the holy Son of God Himself." The three paragraphs at the end of the lesson speak directly to this discussion. Think again of Sisyphus, and ourselves as examples of his situation of futility and despair.

(W-pI.191.9:1) You who perceive yourself as weak and frail, with futile hopes and devastated dreams, born but to die, to weep and suffer pain....

This idea of what our lives amount to is more than familiar to us by now. We are "weak and frail, with futile hopes, and devastated dreams, born but to die, to weep and suffer pain...." Nothing works here. Recall the statement with which Camus began his essay: The only serious philosophical problem is suicide. This appears to be a legitimate response to all Jesus has described, if we forget this is a dream. Jesus continues:

(9:1-2) …hear this: All power is given unto you in earth and Heaven. There is nothing that you cannot do.

This is a reference to the well-known biblical line "All power is given unto me [Jesus] in heaven and in earth" (Matthew 28:18), which here refers to the mind's ability to choose earth or Heaven. When we choose the former, which we did when we decided to be born, our minds also retain the power to choose how we will see it: through the eyes of the ego or the Holy Spirit. There is thus nothing we cannot do because it is our dream. This is not a call to do wonderful and healing things; Jesus is not telling Sisyphus to move the mountain with the power of his mind, which might be a neat psychic trick. The only thing that would bring us the peace of Heaven is to choose it.

(9:3) You play the game of death, of being helpless, pitifully tied to dissolution in a world which shows no mercy to you.

We need to pay attention to these words: "You play the game of death." Life is *our* game. *We* play it and it is *our* choice. However, we certainly do not experience ourselves as playing a game, but we do experience being helpless, tied to dissolution in a merciless world. How, then, can there be hope? If it is true that we play the game of death, who is the *you* that is playing? As Hamlet said: "Ay, there's the rub." The *you* that plays the game is our decision maker, the seat of all power. The *you* that pushes the rock up the mountain has no power. We might have the physical power to do so, but we have no power in the situation, which was decreed by the gods as punishment for sin; our irrevocable fate. Yet Jesus is not inciting us to rebel, nor to appeal to the judges in Hades who made the ruling. Instead, he says: "Let me help you choose again. Let me be your eyes for judging the situation correctly; that this is your dream of sin, guilt, and punishment, and one you can now look at differently."

Therefore, before we awaken from the dream—which would be threatening to all of us—we change the dreams in our experience from nightmares to happy dreams. We may still be helplessly pushing the stone, because we cannot go against the gods, but we are not helpless; the power of our minds can choose to look at the situation in another way: not as a crucifixion, an unjust fate of humiliating and devastating punishment, but as an opportunity to realize that we can transcend the hopelessness of the situation by returning to the source of true power: the mind of the dreamer—*us*.

(9:4) Yet when you accord it mercy, will its mercy shine on you.

When we think merciful thoughts, the merciless world becomes merciful because it is nothing more or less than a projection of the mind's content. If we change the thought, the world will change accordingly —but not necessarily in form. As Jesus told Helen:

> There will not be a change that eyes can see (*The Gifts of God*, p. 117).

What changes is the inner eye with which we see, which is now stated even more clearly:

(10:1) Then let the Son of God awaken from his sleep, and opening his holy eyes, return again to bless the world he made.

Sisyphus but dreams. The pranks he pulled as king were simply dreams, as were the gods' antics. Jesus thus urges us: "Do not try to change the dream, to fix the world. Open your eyes to the truth and gently awaken." And now that our right-minded Sisyphus opens his eyes and sees all this is a dream, and now that he has a companion in his mind with whom he pushes up the stone, he is happy, as Camus observed at the end of his essay. All who visit him in Hades will thus see his joy. His body may still sweat with steam that rises from his effort, but there will be a peace about him. He will look like anyone else pursuing a futile task, but he will "smile more frequently"; his "forehead [will be] serene [and his] eyes...quiet"

(W-pI.155.1:2-3). This, therefore, is how we bless the world. Nothing changes externally—we still behave normally—but now we have a quiet, inner smile and unfurrowed brow. We are not mean or critical, taking out our cruel fate on those around us. Knowing that it ultimately makes no difference what we do with our lives, we are gentle, kind, and peaceful. Nothing has changed but with *whom* our minds are joined.

Surely all would pay lip service to this principle. The problem is that we do not realize that letting Jesus' love flow through us means we need to get ourselves out of the way: our preconceived notions of how things should be; everything we set up as demands of how we and others ought to behave. With this in mind, we revisit a paragraph from Lesson 189, now quoted in full:

> Simply do this: Be still, and lay aside all thoughts of what you are and what God is; all concepts you have learned about the world; all images you hold about yourself. Empty your mind of everything it thinks is either true or false, or good or bad, of every thought it judges worthy, and all the ideas of which it is ashamed. Hold onto nothing. Do not bring with you one thought the past has taught, nor one belief you ever learned before from anything. Forget this world, forget this course, and come with wholly empty hands unto your God (W-pI.189.7).

In other words, we do not live in the past nor fear the future. We thus forget the unjust fate of pushing a rock up a mountain in a perpetual state of futility and hopelessness; nor do we make judgments about our lives: being in Hades is bad; living in Corinth is good. We live in the present, with no thoughts from the past or anticipated future to interfere with our gentle stillness.

From the next paragraph in the same lesson:

> Your part is simply to allow all obstacles that you have interposed between the Son and God the Father to be quietly removed forever. God will do His part in joyful and immediate response. Ask and receive. But do not make demands, nor point the road to God by which He should appear to you. The way to reach Him is merely to let Him be (W-pI.189.8:3-7).

Jesus thus asks us not to make demands to escape our predicament—Get me off this mountain! Take me out of this job! Free me from this relationship!—for that would make it real, obscuring the true problem of our mind's decision for guilt. Similarly, we should not be asking Jesus for help to save the world. How can we save a world that does not exist? Moreover, how could we possibly know what is needed, even if the world were real? The minute we think there is a world to be saved, we become the one in need of saving. We thus save ourselves from this belief by going to the One Who helps us heal the mind and choose again.

Returning to Lesson 191:

(10:2-8) In error it began, but it will end in the reflection of his holiness. And he [the Son of God] **will sleep no more and dream of death. Then join with me today. Your glory is the light that saves the world. Do not withhold salvation longer. Look about the world, and see the suffering there. Is not your heart willing to bring your weary brothers rest?**

When Jesus says to look around the world and see its suffering, he is not speaking of the Middle East, Africa, or the inner city, but the pain that is in everyone —we all are like Sisyphus, forever pushing the boulder of our fate up the mountain of life, only to fail in the end, "wander[ing] on, only to return" (T-19. IV-D.10:8). In other words, Jesus is not talking about the *form* of suffering, but its universal *content*: the suffering we share as aliens in a world we know is not our home, yet not knowing where that home is; and even if we did know, our perceived sin demands the belief that its doors could never be open in welcome.

Nonetheless, no matter what we do, how insignificant, demeaning, or upsetting our lives may be, they remain wonderful opportunities for us to learn we can yet be happy, like Camus' Sisyphus. Once again, we need only be aware of what is truly going on; looking with Jesus at the dream gives us the vision to know it is a dream. Moreover, the world's disturbed dreams are the effect of a disturbed mind that chose the thought of disturbance instead of peace. And so it can choose again and bring rest to God's weary Son.

(11:1-5) They must await your own release. They stay in chains till you are free. They cannot see the mercy of the world until you find it in yourself. They suffer pain until you have denied its hold on you. They die till you accept your own eternal life.

This is certainly not meant to lay guilt trips on us—that others suffer because of us. Rather, it reflects the fact that God's Son is one; its seeming fragments united in one mind, as the next lines reflect:

(11:6-8) You are the holy Son of God Himself. Remember this, and all the world is free. Remember this, and earth and Heaven are one.

The Sonship of God is one. If we are in the hell of judgment, we hold everyone there; similarly, if we forgive, reflecting the peace of Heaven, our healed minds extend to welcome the world. As Jesus says at the end of the text:

> Choose once again if you would take your place among the saviors of the world, or would remain

> in hell, and hold your brothers there (T-31.VIII.
> 1:5; italics omitted).

The choice is ours—to heal or condemn, to see through the eyes of vision or judgment—and what we choose affects the Sonship as one because there is only one mind, not separated or fragmented. Sisyphus' learning to be happy frees the world from imprisonment; not from the gods, but from the mind's thoughts of sin, guilt, and fear.

This is what Jesus means when he says that "salvation of the world depends on me" (W-pI.186). If these lines are understood from the world's perspective, it is difficult to avoid a specialness trip. When we are told that the light of the world is in us and that the world needs us (e.g., W-pI.61-63), it is not the external or specific function that is meant; nor are bodies the referent—we are not dreams that come in mockery (*The Gifts of God*, p. 121). Since the world emanates from the darkened mind of God's one Son, we all need to choose the Holy Spirit's light-filled thought system that indeed saves the world because it heals the mind.

In the text, we are told that the body and ego are parodies and travesties of God's perfect creation, which is spirit (T-24.VII.1:11; 10:9). If Jesus were truly here in a body, God and His Son would be mocked. Our reality, as was Jesus', is outside the dream. Therefore, his love manifested in the dream in a form we call Jesus. However, the world made him part of its dream. We therefore need to be vigilant against doing that with his course. Our teacher is not speaking to us as a body or personality, but only as a mind, asking us to join with him by taking his hand and looking through his eyes from above the battleground. In his vision the world is perceived differently. No matter where we are in life, we will be peaceful. No matter what catastrophic thing has just happened to us or our families, we will be happy because we will know this is a dream. Jesus' love will then flow through our minds, directing what our bodies say and do. This means that even if, in the eyes of the world, we may be busy and helpful, we would remain in the mind's quiet center (T-18.VII.8) and have literally no concern with the world, knowing it exists only within the mind.

To repeat this important point, this is not saying that we should not do things in the world. It is simply saying that what we do is the effect, and our focus should only be on the cause—the mind. Thus Jesus says:

> This is a course in cause and not effect (T-21. VII.7:8).

This is a course in changing our minds about the world, not the world itself. Our failing to recognize this is why everything is always so wrong here, and why even the most well-meaning people are ultimately not helpful. This also explains why utopian visions fail—because people get attached to the form, to the effect. Karl Marx was obviously correct in pointing to greed and inequality as the world's problem. Yet he missed the central point that had nothing to do with economics, but with the greed and inequality—the belief in separate interests—that is in *everyone's* mind, regardless of political points of view. Moreover, we know that everyone has this problem because we all believe we are here, and until this thought is addressed and undone in the mind, the world's suffering will continue.

And so when Jesus speaks of setting the goal (T-17.VI), or he asks us to decide on the day we want (T-30.I), he is not referring to winning the lottery or walking out of a hospital room feeling fine. His point is only our having inner peace: Do we want a day in which we are truly peaceful, or one of stress and conflict? This is why his is a course in cause (the mind), and not effect (behavior), and why its focus is the miracle, which restores "to cause [the mind] the function of causation, not effect" (T-28.II.9:3). The miracle returns to our awareness the fact that it is the mind that causes the world, which is merely its effect. Thus the title, *A Course in Miracles*—a course that has nothing to do with behavior, which is why it should never be taken as a guide for decisions here. The Course's purpose, once again, is only to help us become peaceful, from which our behavior will lovingly flow.

9. "The Real Alternative"

The remainder of our discussion will center on the section "The Real Alternative" from the final chapter of the text (T-31.IV). We quoted from this section earlier (see pp. 41-45), and continue where we left off:

(T-31.IV.3:4-7) Men have died on seeing this [the futility of life's roads]**, because they saw no way except the pathways offered by the world. And learning they led nowhere, lost their hope. And yet this was the time they could have learned their greatest lesson. All must reach this point, and go beyond it.**

Think back to the branching of the road (see p. 59). We go up the vertical line to the splitting of the Y, and then make our choice: to continue with the ego or Jesus—a life of futility and death, or one of happiness that reflects eternal life.

(3:8-10) It is true indeed there is no choice at all within the world. But this is not the lesson in itself. The lesson has a purpose, and in this you come to understand what it is for.

Purpose is one of the central themes in *A Course in Miracles*. What is the purpose of Sisyphus pushing the boulder up the mountain, hoping to get it to the other side, only to have it reach the top and roll down so that he begins again? What is the purpose of our individual lives? We are born but to die; we eat only to eat again; we take a shower only to shower again; we are tired at the end of the day and go to bed, only to wake the next morning to continue the same cycle. What is it all for?

If we think there is a purpose inherent in the world, we are finished. What hope can there be if we come into this world only to leave it? What is the purpose of pushing a rock up a mountain only to have it roll down? Why live an existence of futility and hopelessness? Yet, there is a purpose here, but not what the world sees. The purpose of this discussion, for example, is not to talk about Sisyphus as such, but to see him as a prototype for living in the world. Thus we learn that the world's only purpose is our learning that it has none. This returns us to the mind, for unless we realize we are minds, suicide *is* the only legitimate response to being here, as Camus pointed out.

The world, therefore, is of value because it can reveal to us the futility of trying to find hope here. Reaching that point, we can say, as did Helen and Bill in 1965: "There must be another way." This, then, is the value of all pain, struggle, and torment: to help us realize that this is what life in the body is, whether or not one is born with a silver spoon in one's mouth. To the Holy Spirit, therefore, the world is a classroom in which our thoughts, feelings, and behavior serve to teach us that the only good, noble, and helpful work is healing our minds through forgiveness. And so there is purpose even here, and with a different outcome from the ego's:

> Tolerance for pain may be high, but it is not without limit. Eventually everyone begins to recognize, however dimly, that there *must* be a better way. As this recognition becomes more firmly established, it becomes a turning point. This ultimately reawakens spiritual vision, simultaneously weakening the investment in physical sight. The alternating investment in the two levels of perception is usually experienced as conflict, which can become very acute. But the outcome is as certain as God (T-2.III.3:5-10).

(4:1) Why would you seek to try another road, another person or another place, when you have learned the way the lesson starts, but do not yet perceive what it is for?

The lesson starts with experiencing the futility of our lives. We are Sisyphus, striving mightily yet getting nowhere. At first, on the way up, we conjure up fancy explanations for what we are doing and why it is so important or terrible, perceiving the wonderful or hurtful people who are part of our life situations. This is how the lesson begins, *but that is not what it is for.*

(4:2-5) Its purpose is the answer to the search that all must undertake who still believe there is another answer to be found. Learn now, without despair, there is no hope of answer in the world. But do not judge the lesson that is but begun with this. Seek not another signpost in the world that seems to point to still another road.

Sisyphus' fate is everyone's fate. As much as we attempt to find yet another mountain, another rock, another special relationship, another toy or trophy, it will not matter. We can change the form, but the content of futility remains the same. The workbook says, "Another can be found" (W-pI.170.8:7), and the text speaks of our embarking on "an endless, unrewarding chain of special relationships" (T-15.VII.4:6). We continually seek for something that will work—another relationship, job, location, whatever—but all for nothing, for the world's roads lead nowhere, except the one that leads within: the path of the miracle.

(4:6-7) No longer look for hope where there is none. Make fast your learning now, and understand you but waste time unless you go beyond what you have learned to what is yet to learn.

We have learned that the world is cruel, unfair, and hopeless. Yet, we can learn something more. If we obsess with where we are and what is wrong, or exult in what we have, we will never move beyond those lessons to the real one, never moving beyond form to the content. This, then, is the purpose of *A Course in Miracles*: to lead us from the world of bodies to the mind, so we may choose again.

Within the mind there are only two choices: Either we look through the eyes of separation, specialness, and guilt, or through the eyes of forgiveness, healing, and peace. There is nothing else, which means it makes no difference what we do; all that matters, once again, is *with whom* we do it. To repeat, this does not mean that we not do things well, efficiently, and to the best of our ability. Why would we *not* want to? With no guilt in our minds, such helpful behavior will automatically occur, for we would be responsible only to love. Whatever form it takes, whatever our expertise, training, and role—it will be filled with the love that flows through us. No matter how many thousands of times we push the boulder up the mountain, we will be at peace.

(4:8) For from this lowest point will learning lead to heights of happiness, in which you see the purpose of the lesson shining clear, and perfectly within your learning grasp.

Jesus is telling us we can be free of all pain and despair. The process can be likened to taking off in an airplane when the weather is stormy. As we ascend through the dark clouds and beyond, the sun suddenly appears. Jesus is thus urging us not to remain on the lower levels of the ego's world, where there is only suffering and disappointment. Raising ourselves with him above the battleground, we pass through the clouds of guilt, as he says in the workbook:

> Try to pass the clouds by whatever means appeals to you. If it helps you, think of me holding your hand and leading you. And I assure you this will be no idle fantasy (W-pI.70.9:2-4).

Jesus asks us to let him guide us through the clouds of guilt, specialness, and futility, for thus he lifts us into the sunlight of vision. Our lessons of forgiveness will shine clear, leading us to the heights of happiness.

The problem, however, is that we do not believe Jesus. And thus we demandingly throw our temper tantrums: "I want you down here with me. I want you to bring the sun where I am. I do not want to go to you." We stomp and scream, rant and rave, furious that he does not do what we want. Moreover, on some level we know Jesus cannot come into the world, for he is not of it—he cannot come where there is nothing. He cannot enter *our* dreams, fantasies, or psychoses, for they were specifically made to exclude him and his love.

Yet, Jesus keeps reaching to us, asking that we take his hand that will lead us through the clouds to the light. In the text, he tells us that clouds have no power;

they cannot even keep a button from falling through them (T-18.IX.6). And so, in effect, he says: "I will take you through your guilt, which is nothing—its clouds are not solid walls of granite. You could be happy even pushing a boulder, day in and day out, getting nowhere. For if you learn to do it with me, you will be happy and peaceful, having learned there is no hierarchy of illusions (T-23.II.2:3)." Therefore, we can be living what appear to be meaningless lives, or lives we may judge as meaningful, like teaching *A Course in Miracles*, and it will make no difference to us. We will have recognized that everything is the same, for illusions are but illusions. This is why miracles have no order of difficulty (T-1.I.1:1). The only thing that is now different, to say it one more time, is *with whom* we think and act. *That* is the lesson this course would teach.

(5:1) Who would be willing to be turned away from all the roadways of the world, unless he understood their real futility?

Jesus wants us to realize the futility of our Sisyphean life. Whenever we think of our daily lives, we should think of our Greek hero and the pointlessness and meaninglessness of his fate. Yet we can still be happy. We then need to see how resistant we are to happiness. To be sure, we want to be happy on our terms, such as having Jesus come into our dream and meet our self-defined needs. Recall our earlier quoted line:

> Thought [or Word] cannot be made into flesh…
> (T-8.VII.7:4).

Spirit does not and cannot enter the world because there is no world; and if it could, it would be as insane as we—going to a place that is nowhere, in which there is nothing.

Since Jesus is not in our dream, though he calls to us from outside it, students of his course are sorely tempted to bring him to their world and thus make *A Course in Miracles* say things it does not mean. Jesus does not try to make our external predicaments better, but rather wants us to realize that there is no way to make them better because they were made precisely not to get better. That purpose is their cause. *Ideas leave not their source*: the source of everything that is wrong with the world is the wish not to have anything go well here. Yet we can leave the ego's source in the mind and choose another one, as we now read:

(5:2) Is it not needful that he should begin with this, to seek another way instead?

We begin by recognizing the futility of our lives here. The world may call this pessimism, yet it is anything but. It is truth. How could it be pessimistic to say nothing works here, since nothing does? Indeed, it is psychotic to think this world works. And so Jesus is asking us to be realistic, as he calls a spade a spade: "Look at the world for what it is. You can escape, but not by running away from it. Instead, join me in rising above it to the mind, seeing its insanity and choosing the sane response of Atonement." Herein lies our hope, as Lesson 226 reminds us:

> If I so choose, I can depart this world entirely. It is not death which makes this possible, but it is change of mind about the purpose of the world. If I believe it has a value as I see it now, so will it still remain for me. But if I see no value in the world as I behold it, nothing that I want to keep as mine or search for as a goal, it will depart from me. For I have not sought for illusions to replace the truth.

> *Father, my home awaits my glad return. Your Arms are open and I hear Your Voice. What need have I to linger in a place of vain desires and of shattered dreams, when Heaven can so easily be mine?* (W-pII.226)

(5:3) For while he sees a choice where there is none, what power of decision can he use?

Here is the first mention in this section of the "power of decision," an extremely important theme: "While he sees a choice where there is none, what power of decision can he use?" Our lesson is the mind's power to choose to be in or out of the dream— not to choose any particular one. There is no power in choosing between two dreams, for that is the choice between illusions. Our true power lies in choosing between truth and illusion: to remain asleep or to awaken; to return to the mind or to remain in the body.

(5:4-5) The great release of power must begin with learning where it really has a use. And what decision has power if it be applied in situations without choice?

"Situations without choice" refers to anything in the world. Choosing between murder and being murdered, our pain and another's suffering, special hate and special love is not a true choice. However, choosing between specialness and forgiveness *is*. The ego negates the mind's power by giving the illusion of choice where there is none—i.e., the body. Once again, living in a palace at the foot of the mountain or pushing the rock up the mountain is no choice at all. Pleasure and pain may look and feel different, but looks and feelings lie. They can indeed be strong, but that does not make them real. In fact, their strength can help us recognize they are not of the body but the mind. One may even say that the stronger our feelings, the more we can see that they are part of the ego's strategy to confuse us, making us mindless.

Thus Jesus teaches us in the manual, in the context of sickness and healing:

> Healing must occur in exact proportion to which the valuelessness of sickness is recognized. One need but say, "There is no gain at all to me in this" and he is healed. But to say this, one first must recognize certain facts. First, it is obvious that decisions are of the mind, not of the body. If sickness is but a faulty problem-solving approach, it is a decision. And if it is a decision, it is the mind and not the body that makes it. The resistance to recognizing this is enormous, because the existence of the world as you perceive it depends on the body being the decision maker. Terms like "instincts," "reflexes" and the like represent attempts to endow the body with non-mental motivators. Actually, such terms merely state or describe the problem. They do not answer it (M-5.II.1).

Therefore, whenever we feel something strongly, we know there is a thought in the mind we should be looking at. Perception must lie, because it tells us there is a world to be perceived and felt, the body being its instrument of deceit. And since feelings seem to come from the body, we know they lie. This does not mean we should not pay attention to them. Quite the contrary; we should. Thus even though we need not accept feelings as truth, they can yet point us to the truth of the mind's decision-making power to choose between the ego and Holy Spirit, Who tells us that the body cannot be trusted: it sees, hears, smells, tastes, and touches what is not there. So why go to it for help? Earlier, in fact, Jesus tells us not to ask the one thing in all the universe—the ego, and therefore the body—that does not know, to tell us what reality is (T-20.III.7).

We therefore need to remember the body's role of deceit, and then apply this purpose to whatever situations we are in, realizing how self-defeating, not to mention self-destructive, our lives are. We must see that no meaningful choice is possible here. To do A or B is not meaningful; but to do A or B with Jesus *is*. This is Sisyphus' lesson: to recognize that choosing out of anger, depression, or fear is no real choice. However, choosing out of anger *or* peace is meaningful choice. Trying to change our external situation for something better makes no sense, for the body cannot be made better or worse: *an illusion is an illusion is an illusion.*

(6:1) The learning that the world can offer but one choice, no matter what its form may be, is the beginning of acceptance that there is a real alternative instead.

The real alternative lies between choosing the ego or Holy Spirit—choosing to remain in the dream and act within it, or choosing to stand back and watch ourselves as dream figures. This alone is a meaningful choice.

(6:2) To fight against this step is to defeat your purpose here.

Our purpose here is to learn that there is a real alternative: there is a mind that chooses, and we are the dreamer of the dream and not the dream figure. Given the disastrous consequences, fighting this learning is simply silly.

(6:3-5) You did not come to learn to find a road the world does not contain. The search for different pathways in the world is but the search for different forms of truth. And this would *keep* the truth from being reached.

We find in these statements echoes of the first law of chaos, which states that not only is there a hierarchy of illusions, but also that truth is relative (T-23.II.2-3). Yet how can that be? We may know truth in different ways, but there remains only the oneness of truth, as in the famous Hindu statement: "Truth is one. The sages know it by many names." There are not many truths, because there is no truth in the world of illusion. This, then, is the only true statement one can make about the world: no truth exists here, for an illusion cannot express reality.

(7:1-2) Think not that happiness is ever found by following a road away from it. This makes no sense, and cannot be the way.

Happiness can be found only in its home in the right mind. Therefore, as long as we devote our attention to external situations, to the extent to which we lose our peace over it we know something is wrong. When we are right-minded, no energy is invested in the world. Love being extended through us requires no effort on our part. It is only when we resist this love that we rely on our own power, and *this* is effortful. Thus if we struggle, if there is tension or anxiety— regardless of what we do—we know we have been listening to the ego. If Sisyphus is now happy, it is because he is pushing the rock effortlessly. No matter its heaviness and his weakness in comparison, he would not experience true effort. He would be at peace at the beginning, on the way up, and while watching the rock roll down the mountain. He will have realized that what makes a difference is *with whom* he is doing the pushing.

As Jesus tells us repeatedly, we always choose between our weakness and the strength of Christ in us (e.g., T-31.VIII.2:3). The world calls the ego's weakness strength: "Look at the mighty things *I* have accomplished, the wonderful things *I* do, how hard *I* work, the people *I* help, the wise things *I* say and write." The *I* is the clue there is a problem, for it means it is only the ego that speaks.

(7:3) To you who seem to find this course to be too difficult to learn, let me repeat that to achieve a goal you must proceed in its direction, not away from it.

If our goal is peace, we can only find it by going toward it, which means returning to the mind. If, on the other hand, the goal is to defend against peace, resisting it by indulging our specialness and reinforcing our separate identities, we will proceed in the direction of the world and body. We first decide our goal, and then choose the teacher who will lead us to it. If therefore our goal is peace, and the "judges in Hades" condemn us to a Sisyphean fate as justified punishment for our misdeeds, we will nonetheless see this as means to achieve our end. No matter what we do, vision sees the situation as the way to remember that the power of decision rests within the mind, and we do not interpret the external as punishment for sin. As the workbook says: "I could see peace instead of this" (W-pI.34); we can be peaceful instead of being resentful and despairing. The choice is ours, and this is the lesson.

Importantly, this approach does not make us passive in the world, nor does it mean that we do nothing here. It means only that we are passive to the ego and active to the Holy Spirit. We may indeed be quite active behaviorally, if love so guides us, but we will no longer experience ourselves as the actors, being but vehicles through whom love flows. It is therefore not *we* who are the doers. Thus there will be, again, no effort, fatigue, or investment in the outcome; no high when something we judge as good happens, or low if something we judge as bad happens—everything will be perceived as the same. Recall the New Year's prayer from the text:

> Make this year different by making it all the same (T-15.XI.10:11).

We make every relationship, situation, and world event the same in terms of our response: a quiet calm. If there is no hierarchy of illusions, there can be no hierarchy of responses. If we listen to the Holy Spirit, we will only feel happy and be at peace. If we listen to the ego, we will only feel miserable, and then try to make others miserable as well, holding them responsible for our unhappiness. This could include *A Course in Miracles* itself, which we would be tempted to blame for our own inability to learn it.

(7:4) And every road that leads the other way will not advance the purpose to be found.

If we say we want to be peaceful, yet keep looking for Jesus to fix our world and bodies, we will continually be frustrated for we will have chosen a means that can never take us to the end. Two parallel sections in the text, "The Consistency of Means and End" (T-20.VII) and "Setting the Goal" (T-17.VI) help us see that if we truly desire peace, we will see everything that happens—regardless of how the world judges it—as a means of helping us achieve our goal. We will have learned that neither salvation nor distress comes from outside—only from the mind's decision for Jesus or the ego.

(7:5-7) If this be difficult to understand, then is this course impossible to learn. But only then. For otherwise, it is a simple teaching in the obvious.

This is Jesus' way of saying to us: "Please do not tell me this is a difficult course. Rather, it is a course to which *you* are very resistant, which is why it seems difficult. Therefore it is not *A Course in Miracles* that is the problem, but what you are doing with it. Resistance to the truth is difficult, as is fighting against it."

And so Jesus' words will mean nothing if we do not apply them to our current situations so that we can see how the way we live ensures our not accepting the means he offers to reach the end, which can only be due to our fear of that end. Being afraid of peace, we do not choose the road that will get us there. As a result, we resent our fate, as one can imagine Sisyphus doing; pointing to the futility and hopelessness of a life that is not his doing. When, however, we rise above judgment to the level of vision, we embrace this life as a classroom, recognizing that this is how we learn our lessons. Thus the means of forgiveness becomes bathed in light, as is our goal of truth. In the *Psychotherapy* pamphlet, Jesus urges therapists to do the same thing—give up judgment (P-3.II.6:1; 7:1)—at which point "the room becomes a temple, and the street a stream of stars…" (P-2.VII.8:4).

Everything then shifts. Sisyphus pushes his boulder up the mountain surrounded by stars and a radiant light. His face is joyful, not because the situation has changed, but because *he* has changed. He has not tried to change his situation by, for example, approaching the inhabitants of Hades to promote an insurrection against the gods in protest of their cruelty. If Sisyphus' revolt were to succeed, it is certain that the new rulers would be just as cruelly egocentric as the ones he over-threw, because he and his band of followers would not have taught the only lesson they truly wanted to learn: nothing in the world has power to make them happy or unhappy.

(8:1-2) There *is* a choice that you have power to make when you have seen the real alternatives.

Until that point is reached you have no choice, and you can but decide how you would choose the better to deceive yourself again.

This describes our lives. We keep trying to make things work, or work better, instead of first accepting where we are and trying to make our thought system better. When we have become right-minded, we will not see situations as capable of making us glad or sad. However, chances are that if there is no anger or guilt, our situation will probably change for the better, and will certainly change in our experience for it will no longer be motivated by self-hate or resentment. When hate is gone, all that remains is love, and only then can any behavioral intervention be truly caring and self-less. Yet when we focus on wanting to change the external instead of simply accepting where we and others are, nothing truly changes because we end up merely manipulating the form, while the underlying thoughts of separation remain. We therefore need to continually focus on the power of our minds to choose, not between illusions, but between illusions and truth. This is our only purpose here, summarized in this next line:

(8:3) This course attempts to teach no more than that the power of decision cannot lie in choosing different forms of what is still the same illusion and the same mistake.

This is Jesus' message in his course, said at the beginning of the text, all the way through, and again at its close, not to mention in the workbook and manual: the power of our decision does not lie in choosing among differing illusions, but in choosing between them and the truth. This is done by bringing the darkness of our hate to the light of his love; we bring our concerns, and feelings of anguish, despair, and hopelessness to the source of hope in the mind. That is why, to repeat it still again, to ask Jesus to help us in the world denies the central teaching of *A Course in Miracles*. If we persist in approaching our world this way, we will never learn its simple lessons—to be learned by the mind, where the power of decision rests. We do not learn in the world or body, nor on Sisyphus' mountain, all of which Jesus and the Holy Spirit know nothing about. They know only about the mind's guilt, resentment, and sense of futility, and their correction by forgiveness.

(8:4) All choices in the world depend on this; you choose between your brother and yourself, and you will gain as much as he will lose, and what you lose is what is given him.

This reflects the reigning principle of the ego thought system—*one or the other*: you win, I lose; you die, I live; you have it, I take it from you. This is

124

the law of the world because it is the law of the ego's mind that gave rise to it: God or the ego. Thus we choose between our Father and our self, and will gain as much as He loses. We believe that He lost His creative power because we usurped it; He lost His life because we now have it—we live because He died in the instant of ultimate sacrifice.

Thus everything in the world, from the dawning of time until its dissolution, is a fragmentary shadow of the ontological thought of what we thought we did to our Creator. We therefore do not love others for the Christ in them, but for what they can do for us. We need others to lose something of themselves so we can have it. We pretend to love them, but indeed hate them for the sin we do not want to see in ourselves. We therefore steal their innocence, enabling us to have it at their expense, for they now possess our projected sin, which leaves us sinless and happy. Needless to say, others believe they have done the same thing to us. We thus act out with each other what we believe occurred in the original moment of separation, relived over and over and over again.

(8:5) How utterly opposed to truth is this, when all the lesson's purpose is to teach that what your brother loses *you* have lost, and what he gains is what is given *you*.

The lesson's purpose is that we are one, a oneness that exists in the mind, not the body:

> Minds are joined; bodies are not (T-18.VI.3:1).

Bodies may seem to join in hate, but they are each separate and cannot truly join. In fact, we hate others in order to keep the illusion of separation alive and well. The Holy Spirit's truth, however, is not *one or the other*, but *together, or not at all* (T-19.IV-D.12:8): If you have it, I must, too—if I have made you guilty, I am guilty as well; if I have seen the face of Christ in you, I share His innocence. It cannot be that we are different. The ego, on the other hand, believes in differences and hierarchies of illusions. It holds that there are worthwhile functions in the world such as saving lives, and worthless ones such as hopelessly pushing a boulder up a mountain. Yet Jesus teaches that an illusion remains an illusion: one is the same as a thousand; multiplying zero by one or a thousand still results in zero. In Heaven we are One as Christ; on earth we are one as egos, as well as in the right-minded correction.

The notion of *one or the other* arose with the belief we separated from God. We made the world to hide from this fact, and then believed God was going to separate from us because He was angry. We thus projected responsibility for the separation, proclaiming: "I am not the one who betrayed God by leaving Him;

He betrayed His Son by leaving me." We thus write our individual scripts that we be born as innocent infants, so that anything that happens is not our fault—it was done *to* us. And so our parents abandoned and abused us, were cruel, insensitive, and unkind; we were not that way to them. After all, who could blame a five-day-old infant? The problem, however, is that we remain that infant, always denying our guilt, protesting our innocence, and making everyone else guilty—all because we believe we did that with God.

And now the correction:

(9:1-2) He has not left His Thoughts! But you forgot His Presence and remembered not His Love.

One way of defining our true Identity is to say we are a Thought in the Mind of God, Who did not leave us; nor did we leave Him. In our dream, however, we forgot His Presence when we seemed to choose against His Love.

(9:3) No pathway in the world can lead to Him, nor any worldly goal be one with His.

Yet this is what most religions and spiritual paths attempt, setting up worldly pathways in elaborate forms and rituals that will lead back to God, when in fact the road to Heaven is simple: leave the illusory world and go within. We may do things here—for example, studying this course and doing its work-book—but these are simply aids. Any true spiritual path moves us beyond the forms to the mind's content of love.

(9:4) What road in all the world will lead within, when every road was made to separate the journey from the purpose it must have unless it be but futile wandering?

Our right-minded purpose in being here is to return to the mind—above the battleground—so we can change it, rather than attempting to change the world: its situations, relationships, and bodies. We recognize the teacher we have chosen—the ego or Jesus—by honestly observing our reactions. Are we tense, angry, resentful, expectant of a certain out-come; or peaceful, content, and benignly indifferent? Are we acting out of a belief in separate or shared interests? Once we believe we can attack others and *not* attack ourselves, we have negated the very cause of peace we espouse. All rebellions and revolutions end up sowing the seeds for the next revolt because the hidden cause of war is never addressed: the mind's decision to be separate; the belief in a thought system of *one or the other* in which people have to be sacri-ficed. The Secretary of Defense remarked at the beginning of a recent war that it just happens that peo-ple get killed, and that's how it is. His comment reflects the notion that some are judged as not being as important as others and can therefore be sacrificed for the greater good of peace. This thinking is based on the idea of separate interests—a hierarchy of life— in which one group benefits at another's expense.

(9:5) All roads that lead away from what you are will lead you to confusion and despair.

We are children of perfect Oneness, in which is found the Oneness of the Sonship. Anything that leads away from our Self—toward the principle of *one or the other*—must lead us to confusion and despair, futility and hopelessness. If Sisyphus pushes the boulder up the mountain with resentment toward the gods, his ego has triumphed. If, however, he pushes the boulder in perfect peace, realizing he is not separate from those he tricked, or the ones who are now punishing him, there will be no loss of peace in him. It all depends on the teacher that is chosen; on the perception of separate versus shared interests.

The right-minded purpose of the world, once we made it, is to have us recognize there is but one Son that made the world, and one Son that will save it. This means that everyone has to be perceived as the same, part of the same Sonship. This practical principle needs to be applied constantly in our everyday lives. Whenever we become annoyed and feel our peace has been taken from us, we can recognize that we have chosen the wrong teacher and thus no longer see the Sonship as one. This makes the outcome of confusion and despair inevitable.

(9:6) Yet has He never left His Thoughts to die, without their Source forever in themselves.

God and Christ remain outside the dream, perfectly united. And so our Source did not leave us to die in the illusion. Since dreams are not His Will, they never happened. Yet within them they seem quite real. As they are governed by the thought of *one or the other*, our birthplace, that is what we live out, justifying our going to war both as individuals and governments. Having an angry thought, even a mild thought of annoyance, is the same as declaring war against a foreign country, for regardless of the intensity of our response, we are believing that others have power to take away our peace, a perception that directs all anger and attack.

(10:1-2) He has not left His Thoughts! He could no more depart from them than they could keep Him out.

God could no more leave us than we could leave Him. Perfect Oneness remains perfectly one. This is the principle of Atonement: nothing happened to separate us from our Source; nothing changed perfect Love. Therefore, there is no need to defend against the guilt from having effected a change that never occurred; hence no need to have a world.

(10:3-4) In unity with Him do they abide, and in Their Oneness Both are kept complete. There is no road that leads away from Him.

Only in dreams are there roads that lead away from God and Christ (the ladder that separation led us down): the roads of sin and guilt, fear and hate, sacrifice and death—all lead to hell, *but only in the dream.*

(10:5-8) A journey from yourself does not exist. How foolish and insane it is to think that there could be a road with such an aim! Where could it go? And how could you be made to travel on it, walking there without your own reality at one with you?

How could we be made to walk on an illusory road —that is why Jesus leads us on "a journey without distance" (T-8.VI.9:7)—when our reality remains at home with God? Sisyphus' mountain does not exist, which is why he could be happy. His is not a road that leads away from God, for he can bring the memory of His Love with him as he labors up the seeming mountain. We all take that memory with us as we live our various roles, and choosing to remember ensures that we fulfill them lovingly and kindly. Whatever the form—helping a family member, friend, or the world —it makes no difference, because we will only be involved with the love in our right minds. Our sphere of attention will have shifted from the world—the futile mountain of our experience—to the mind's love and peace. Accomplishing this shift is the meaning of our relationship with Jesus or the Holy Spirit. This change is everything. It does not necessarily change the externals of our lives, but does change how we perceive them. In other words, this shift from body to mind shifts how we feel within. And so we will smile more frequently and our foreheads will be serene (W-pI.155.1:2-3), for we will have accepted the peace that was always there.

(11:1-4) Forgive yourself your madness, and forget all senseless journeys and all goal-less aims. They have no meaning. You cannot escape from what you are. For God is merciful, and did not let His Son abandon Him.

These sentences can be read on two levels. We cannot escape from what the ego tells us, because we are not there. Yet we also cannot escape from what we are as Christ. Thus, as we go through our daily Sisyphean life, we learn to forgive ourselves for having believed we were like Sisyphus, justified in being angry and resentful because of our hopeless and futile lives that have kept us doing meaningless and irrelevant things, accomplishing nothing. Yet we can truly accomplish everything and be happy if we learn Jesus' lesson. It does not matter why we ended up on the mountain, senselessly pushing the stone. All that matters is that we do it differently now: with Jesus and his peace. This realization is remarkably freeing, for we no longer have to fight the world and its evildoers. Forgiveness thus lifts a tremendous burden from our weary shoulders and we cease the senseless journeys that lead only to death. As we read in the text:

> The journey to the cross should be the last "useless journey" (T-4.in.3:1).

Thus our madness was but a bad dream, a feverish nightmare of despair and loss that was filled with the futility of nothingness. Yet it remains the dream it always was.

(11:5) For what He is be thankful, for in that is your escape from madness and from death.

God's perfect and loving Oneness means He has not left His Thoughts, and They have not left Him. Nothing has changed. Yet our "raucous shrieks" (W-pI.49.4:3)—our anxiety, depression, and self-hate —loudly proclaim: "I did leave God." And then, through projection: "*No, He left me!*" Each time we pout or scream, pounding our chest in defiance or someone else's in anger, we assert: "I exist; I accomplished the impossible. And you cannot tell me I am mistaken." However, there is a wonderfully simple line, infuriating to the ego, that comes after Jesus describes an aspect of the ego system:

And God thinks otherwise (T-23.I.2:7).

This is why we hate God. He thinks otherwise about us, for His Oneness means we do not exist. To believe He did leave us would justify our individual lives, protecting the secret belief that we left Him. We revel, therefore, in His punishing us with a meaningless life because that means we actually sinned. Our rebellion changed God, which means we have power over Him, as did Sisyphus with Zeus and Hades (outsmarting the gods, he forced them to get even), and so our suffering proves we are indeed separated and our thought system real. Thus we cherish authority problems—either defying authority figures or succumbing to them. Their separating, if not abusive, presence in our lives buttresses our argument that separation and sin are real, and demand punishment. Yet recognizing the insanity of this perception is what effects our escape from the futility and hopelessness of our lives, which amount to nothing.

One ego ploy to establish the "truth" of our situation is to compare ourselves with others: they do wonderful work, and look at what we do. It is the height of arrogance and madness to think that what anyone does here means anything. Dreams cannot be meaningful and "love makes no comparisons" (T-24.II.1:2; W-pI.195.4:2). The purpose of this course, therefore, is to help us awaken from the dream and return to the reality of Heaven's Oneness.

(11:6) Nowhere but where He is can you be found.

God is in our mind because the memory of Heaven is there, not in the world of bodies. If the boulder went over the other side of the mountain instead of rolling back down, nothing would change—this is not Heaven. It does not matter what happens in the world, since its problems are not the problem, which is only the *mind's* decision for sin, guilt, hate, and death. If we truly want to end their painful manifestations, we must end their source in the decision-making mind. The loving consequences of our right-minded decision will flow through us, but these are not our concern. We should not put the cart before the horse, effect before its cause.

(11:7) There *is* no path that does not lead to Him.

Even if we push the stone up the mountain forever, it will still lead us to God if we bring the memory of His Love with us. No worldly path in and of itself will lead to Him. We transcend the world's multitudinous paths by taking Jesus with us as we walk. The *form* of the path does not matter—where it seems to go, or how futile it seems to be—if we choose the *content* of forgiveness as our guide: the ultimate message of *A Course in Miracles*. Forgiveness changes everything, not because the external necessarily shifts, but because our minds have shifted from futility to happiness, from the ego to God.

Q: Does anything I do in the world influence my mind? For example, does picking up the Course affect my mind?

A: No. How could anything in the world influence your mind if there is no world? The world can have no effect on you since it has never left its source in your mind. And so, your picking up the Course was the effect of a decision that your mind made, choosing Jesus as its teacher instead of the ego. The form that choice took was for you to study *A Course in Miracles*. Therefore, nothing you do as a seeming person means anything at all. After all, can a puppet change a puppeteer? The puppet or marionette is merely a lifeless piece of painted and clothed wood with strings attached to it. Recall this line from "The Laws of Chaos":

> Can you paint rosy lips upon a skeleton, dress it in loveliness, pet it and pamper it, and make it live? (T-23.II.18:8).

Whatever the puppeteer wants the puppet to do, it does. Unless you are living in the Twilight Zone, the puppet has no effect on the puppeteer. However, what *does* affect the puppeteer is the puppeteer. There is no one else. If you are in a movie theater, and in a crazed state go up to the screen and put a knife through it, you will have no effect on the film running through the projector. Yet if you go to the projection booth and put a knife through the film, you will most definitely see a change on the screen. It is the same with the mind and body. What makes this idea difficult to accept is that our experience tells us that we—the people we think we are—are studying *A Course in Miracles*. We know we have really made progress with this course when we begin to experience the fact that Jesus is not addressing the self we believe ourselves to be, but the mind's decision maker that has chosen to express itself in the form we call our selves, with which we identify so strongly.

Once again, it is difficult not to think that Jesus is talking to us in this book. It is interesting to see how we respond to those passages—and there are many— that say that our eyes do not see and our brains do not think. After all, our experience is certainly that our eyes are reading the words that tell us we are not see-ing, and our brains are thinking the very words that say they cannot think. It is truly a wonderful Zen koan for it sets up a logical paradox we cannot transcend except by becoming *a*logical; i.e., returning to the pre-logical mind that has chosen to be a body, governed by a logical brain we think can think. *A Course in Miracles*, then, helps us break our identification with the ego self so we can return to the decision-making mind, look at the ego's wrong-minded thought system of separation and specialness, and choose differently. We begin by understanding this intellectually, and then over time we are increasingly able to step back—*as a mind*—and observe ourselves choosing to become upset or sick. Those experiences allow us to remember to laugh at the silliness of the tiny, mad idea of separation as it is expressed in our lives. And thus, like our friend Sisyphus, we can become truly happy.

Closing

I close with a lovely poem of Helen's that reflects our book's theme. It is called "Transformation," written down by Helen after an experience such as is described in the poem itself.* Its Easter theme is seen in the poem's closing lines: "By the tomb / The angel stands in shining hopefulness / To give salvation's message: 'Be you free, / And stay not here. Go on to Galilee.'" This symbol of resurrection or rebirth is the answer to "Stabat Mater"—the desolation of standing at the foot of the cross. Taking Jesus' loving hand, we go beyond the cross to the resurrection, awakening at last from the dream of despair and death. This transformation, again, has nothing to do with the external, but our inner shift allows us to perceive the world through the joy-filled eyes of Christ's holy vision. Our journey from futility to happiness is complete, and we are home at last.

Here now is Helen's poem (*The Gifts of God*, p. 64):

---

* For the full story of the poem, please see my *Absence from Felicity: The Story of Helen Schucman and Her Scribing of "A Course in Miracles,"* pp. 392-93.

Transformation

It happens suddenly. There is a Voice
That speaks one Word, and everything is changed.

You understand an ancient parable
That seemed to be obscure. And yet it meant
Exactly what it said. The trivial
Enlarge in magnitude, while what seemed large
Resumes the littleness that is its due.
The dim grow bright, and what was bright before
Flickers and fades and finally is gone.
All things assume the role that was assigned
Before time was, in ancient harmony
That sings of Heaven in compelling tones
Which wipe away the doubting and the care
All other roles convey. For certainty
Must be of God.
                    It happens suddenly,
And all things change. The rhythm of the world
Shifts into concert. What was harsh before
And seemed to speak of death now sings of life,
And joins the chorus to eternity.
Eyes that were blind begin to see, and ears
Long deaf to melody begin to hear.
Into the sudden stillness is reborn
The ancient singing of creation's song,
Long silenced but remembered. By the tomb
The angel stands in shining hopefulness
To give salvation's message: "Be you free,
And stay not here. Go on to Galilee.

INDEX OF REFERENCES TO *A COURSE IN MIRACLES*

text

text (cont.)

text (cont.)

workbook for students

workbook for students (cont.)

manual for teachers

Psychotherapy: Purpose, Process and Practice

The Gifts of God

Foundation for A COURSE IN MIRACLES®

Kenneth Wapnick *received his Ph.D. in Clinical Psychology in 1968 from Adelphi University. He was a close friend and associate of Helen Schucman and William Thetford, the two people whose joining together was the immediate stimulus for the scribing of A COURSE IN MIRACLES. Kenneth had been involved with A COURSE IN MIRACLES since 1973, writing, teaching, and integrating its principles with his practice of psychotherapy. He was on the Executive Board of the Foundation for Inner Peace, publishers of A COURSE IN MIRACLES.*

In 1983, with his wife Gloria, he began the Foundation for A COURSE IN MIRACLES, and in 1984 this evolved into a Teaching and Healing Center in Crompond, New York, which was quickly outgrown. In 1988 they opened the Academy and Retreat Center in upstate New York. In 1995 they began the Institute for Teaching Inner Peace through A COURSE IN MIRACLES, an educational corporation chartered by the New York State Board of Regents. In 2001 the Foundation moved to Temecula, California, and shifted its emphasis to electronic teaching. After Dr. Wapnick's death in 2013, it was decided to move to a smaller facility, which happened in October 2018 when the Foundation moved to Henderson, Nevada.

The following is Kenneth's and Gloria's vision of the Foundation:

In our early years of studying *A Course in Miracles,* as well as teaching and applying its principles in our respective professions of psychotherapy, and teaching and school administration, it seemed evident that this was not the simplest of thought systems to understand. This was so not only in the intellectual grasp of its teachings, but perhaps more importantly in the application of these teachings to our personal lives. Thus, it appeared to us from the beginning that the Course lent itself to teaching, parallel to the ongoing teachings of the Holy Spirit in the daily opportunities within our relationships, which are discussed in the early pages of the manual for teachers.

One day several years ago while Helen Schucman and I (Kenneth) were discussing these ideas, she shared a vision that she had had of a teaching center as a white temple with a gold cross atop it. Although it was clear that this image was symbolic, we understood it to be representative of what the teaching center was to be: a place where the person of Jesus and his message in *A Course in Miracles* would be manifest. We have sometimes seen an image of a light-house shining its light into the sea, calling to it those passers-by who sought it. For us, this light is the Course's teaching of forgiveness, which we would hope to share with those who are drawn to the Foundation's form of teaching and its vision of *A Course in Miracles*.

This vision entails the belief that Jesus gave the Course at this particular time in this particular form for several reasons. These include:

1) the necessity of healing the mind of its belief that attack is salvation; this is accomplished through forgiveness, the undoing of our belief in the reality of separation and guilt.

2) emphasizing the importance of Jesus and/or the Holy Spirit as our loving and gentle Teacher, and developing a personal relationship with this Teacher.

3) correcting the errors of Christianity, particularly where it has emphasized suffering, sacrifice, separation, and sacrament as being inherent in God's plan for salvation.

Our thinking has always been inspired by Plato (and his mentor Socrates), both the man and his teachings. Plato's Academy was a place where serious and thoughtful people came to study his philosophy in an atmosphere conducive to their learning, and then returned to their professions to implement what they were taught by the great philosopher. Thus, by integrating abstract philosophical ideals with experience, Plato's school seemed to be the perfect model for the teaching center that we directed for so many years.

We therefore see the Foundation's principal purpose as being to help students of *A Course in Miracles* deepen their understanding of its thought system, conceptually and experientially, so that they may be more effective instruments of Jesus' teaching in their own lives. Since teaching forgiveness without experiencing it is empty, one of the Foundation's specific goals is to help facilitate the process whereby people may be better able to know that their own sins are forgiven and that they are truly loved by God. Thus is the Holy Spirit able to extend His Love through them to others.